th

n

$th.$

l_2

OFFSHORE LIVING
&
INVESTING

YOUR MONEY & YOUR LIFE

David A. Tanzer, Esq.

COPYRIGHT PROTECTED AND REPRINT PERMISSION

OFFSHORE LIVING & INVESTING – YOUR MONEY AND YOUR LIFE

THE ULTIMATE TAX PLAN: DENOUNCING U.S. CITIZENSHIP

DON'T LEAVE YOUR SOCIAL SECURITY BENEFITS BEHIND

Acknowledgements

Iextend my deepest appreciation and sincere gratitude to a very long list of people for which I am deeply indebted to enable me to share the ideas in this book. Without their energetic commitments to encourage me to clarify the material on these pages, it would still only be another goal waiting to be realized.

Running the risk of offending many contributors to the ideas expressed in this book, I first thank my wife Susan for putting up with my idiosyncrasies driving us to become what seems to some as international gypsies as we explore the world we have only just begun to understand. And too, thanks to our oldest daughter Alyssa who now pursues her quest to become a third generation lawyer, on her terms, but only after her threats to the contrary; to our youngest daughter Alexa as she explores what seems to be unlimited boundaries with a heart of gold; and both destined to do great things. All three have shared in the same dreams and desires as I to become international citizens of the world, continuing in the pursuit of cultural understanding. Each of their dreams has served to keep me motivated to explore and understand.

My long time best friend "Omar" (he insisted I not disclose his real name) from America, who has shared with me many memorable moments of friendship and camaraderie, and also in the challenge of helping me communicate the sometimes difficult concepts and ideas found in this book. We have grown together in our business and professional interests for almost 25 years, and at times we disagreed to an extreme, serving to crystallize my thoughts and ideas.

And to my good Kiwi mate, Miles-Agmen Smith, who with me enjoys tasting fine wines of the world, and whose legal background and expertise assisted our family settling into New Zealand after we first landed in the Land of the Long White Cloud. I thank him too for resisting proofreading changes from my American-English to his British roots of Queens-English; and whose contribution to help our third generation lawyer find her feet is greatly appreciated.

To my sister Cathy, I thank for helping to inspire this book with her never ending questions, and for reminding me that you can't make everyone happy.

Special thank you and a hug to Lorain Sviridov, when at the age of 7 she photographed the outstanding cover image of her beautiful mother, Tatiana, a very special lady; and to Shawn at Most4U Design Group for capturing the magic moment on the dustcover of this book for all the world to enjoy forever.

But most of all, I thank the many clients and friends who inquires are often reflected in pages of this book. For without them, I would cease to be challenged. As is often the case, I learn through them.

Dedication

This book is dedicated to the individual thinkers of the world willing to stand out as the lone wolves....... even if no one listens in the dark of the night.

Any person willing to give up freedom for security deserves neither.
Thomas Jefferson

Introduction

First, we survived being born to mothers who smoked and/or drank while they carried us. They took aspirin, ate blue cheese dressing and didn't get tested for diabetes.

Then after that trauma, our baby cribs were covered with bright colored lead-based paints. We had no childproof lids on medicine bottles, doors or cabinets and when we rode our bikes, we wore no helmets, not to mention the risks some of us took hitchhiking.

As children, we would ride in cars with no seat belts or air bags. Riding in the back of a pickup for some of us on a warm summer day was a special treat.

We drank water from the garden hose and *not* from a bottle. We shared one soft drink with four friends, from one bottle, and no one actually died from this.

We ate cupcakes, bread and butter and drank soda pop with sugar in it, but we weren't overweight because we were always busy playing outside.

We would leave home in the morning and play all day, as long as we were back when the streetlights came on. No one was able to reach us all day. And we were OK.

We would spend hours building our go-carts out of scraps and then ride down the hill, only to find out we forgot the brakes. After running into the bushes a few times, we learned to solve the problem.

We did not have Playstations, Nintendo's, X-boxes; no video games, no txting, no 999 channels on cable, no DVDs, no video tape movies, no surround sound, no cell phones, no personal computers, no Internet or Internet chat rooms..........we had friends and we went outside and found them!

We fell out of trees, got cut, broke bones and teeth and there were no lawsuits from these accidents. We made up games with sticks and tennis balls and ate worms and although we were told it would happen, we did not put out very many eyes, nor did the worms live in us forever.

We rode bikes or walked to a friend's house and knocked on the door or rang the bell, or just walked in and talked to them!

Little league had tryouts and not everyone made the team. Those who didn't had to learn to deal with disappointment. Imagine that!

The idea of a parent bailing us out of jail if we broke the law was unheard of. They actually sided with the law!

This generation has produced some of the best risk-takers, problem solvers and inventors ever! And the past 50 years has experienced an explosion of innovation and new ideas.

We had freedom, failure, success and responsibility, and we learned how to deal with it all.

And you and I are one of them! *Congratulations!*

And all this before the plaintiff tort lawyers and the government do-gooders regulated our lives, for our own good. Kind of makes you want to do something special today, doesn't it?

Thank you friends, family and unknown authors for these contributions.

What has gone wrong in our society when common sense is set aside and is replaced by rules and regulations controlling every facet of our lives by people who don't know us, or know even less than we do?

For some looking beyond their backyard for a better life means going "offshore." For others looking to reinvent themselves means finding new horizons and challenges. Whoever first said *"the world is your oyster"* was wise beyond their years. Even with all the problems we see in the news, on the Internet or in hardcopy, the world still offers an exciting and wonderful opportunity for those willing to open their eyes, explore, learn and play outside their comfort zone.

Some people are fearful that if they reach out beyond their grasp, they might fail. For me, my only fear is that if I don't keep reaching beyond what is in my grasp, exploring new worlds, I will fail.

The offshore world offers an exciting opportunity to learn, explore and grow. Many of the topics covered in this book grew out of friends, family and client's inquiries over recent years. Not everyone looking to go offshore will be confronted by the same issues or all of the issues found herein. But for those looking to broaden their understanding as to what "going offshore" means, this will provide an excellent starting point.

Some sections offer summaries and examples, and a few are unapologetically technical, since that is the very nature of the topic. You can easily read or pass over sections not of interest and gain value by reading those sections having meaning to you.

So open your eyes to a better understanding of the offshore world.

And remember, life is not a dress rehearsal, it is the real deal. Live your dreams to the fullest.

CUTTING MOTHER'S APRON STRINGS

When all think alike, no one is thinking very much.
Walter Lippmann

CHAPTER ONE

Is Going Offshore Legal?

How many times have you thought about creating a new life "offshore"? What do you need to know before you move your money, or your family, or both, away from the perceived safety of mother homeland? Is it a realistic option? Is it complicated?

First, a definition of "offshore." Offshore is anything that is not "onshore" within the boundaries of where you presently live. In other words, any place outside of your homeland is considered "offshore." Every country is offshore to every other place. And each jurisdiction has its own ever-changing laws and political aspirations.

With over 190 countries worldwide, and over 6 Billion people globally, there is a *huge* world outside the boundaries of where you call home. How many of those countries, capitals, and leaders can you name or locate on a map right now? To how many have you traveled? And how many cultures do you understand and respect?

If the world was reduced to a village of only 100 people, proportionately, the village would consist of 60 Asians, 12 Europeans, 5 U.S. and Canadians, and 8 Latin Americans. Forty nine would be female and 51 would be male, with 82 non-whites and 18 whites. Eighty nine would be heterosexual and 11 homosexual.

Amazingly, 5 of the villagers would control 32% of the entire world's wealth, and all of them would be U.S. citizens. What's more, 80 would live in substandard housing, 24 would not have any electricity, 67 would be unable to read, 50 would be malnourished and 1 dying of starvation. Thirty three of our inhabitants would be without access to safe water and 1 would have H.I.V. One would be near death, 2 near birth, 7 would have access to the Internet, and 1 (only one) would have a college education.

If you look at our village of 100 from this point of view, the world takes on a whole new meaning.

And if you woke up healthy this morning, you should be happier than the 1 millionth person that would not live to see the end of next week.

If you have never experienced a war, the cage of imprisonment, the agony of torture, or a famine, you are better off than 500 million persons in this world. And if you can attend a church, synagogue or mosque without any fear or threats of the consequences, you are better situated than almost 3 billion people worldwide.

If there is a meal in your refrigerator, you are dressed in clothes and shoes, live with a roof over your head, you are better off than 75% of the world population. And if you have a bank account with money in your pocket you belong to 8% of the well-provided people in the world. Since you can read this text, you do not belong to the 2 billion people who can not read.

It is true the world is a very different place and offers much to discover and learn. Maybe this is why moving capital and people offshore is so "foreign" to so many people, especially Americans. It shouldn't be, but I hear the same question repeatedly by those I consider educated and well-reasoned people: Is it legal to go "offshore?"

I believe the answer is that too many of the western cultures, particularly Americans, live sheltered and uninformed as to what is really happening in the rest of the world. The major news media doesn't help, since they only report "newsworthy" local news or biased "foreign" news which only reflects local interests. Few people actually bother to understand the rest of the world and what makes it tick... or worse yet, care. Instead, most are busy with daily activities, growing old, getting fat, and working more so they can consume an endless supply of goods and services... naturally, present company excluded.

This book is for the rest of us who believe the world is a precious oyster... for those of us with a genuine curiosity to travel, learn or invest outside of our home country. We yearn to learn what makes the world and its inhabitants tick. We live with interest and respect for our neighbor's way of life – at least we try to understand – and look to broaden our horizons for new opportunities and a fresh or better quality of living.

Mobility today is commonplace. According to the U.S. Census Bureau, we are not alone, in that during 2002 to 2003 some 200,000 U.S. citizens emigrated. While that number represents a small portion of the 300 million American population, it is still a very large number. And according to U.N. calculations, a total of 3% of the world population – some 180,000,000 (equal to two-thirds of the U.S. population) – are immigrants. That makes population mobility a very common event.

At one time people crossed artificial political boundaries with ease, and with minimal, if any, restrictions. Passports as we know them are actually a creation of this last century, and were originally used only as a diplomatic introduction. They were never designed or intended to be "permission slips" to satisfy bureaucratic busybodies.... unfortunately, those days are long gone.

The question "Is it *really* legal to go offshore?" lingers for many.

And too, an incorrect impression often comes about due to a series of planned, unjustified attacks on offshore financial activity over the years by the U.S. IRS, the U.K. Customs and Revenue, Canada Revenue, the Australian Taxation Office, and other tax collectors in "high tax" nations. Needless to say, this has sowed confusion and fear in the minds of people who have shied away from going offshore. It looks like the tax collectors achieved the results they wanted.

Yes, there are definitely reporting requirements and tax laws you need to comply with when you "go offshore." But there are <u>no</u> - repeat - <u>no</u> outright and explicit prohibitions against American, Australian, British, Canadian or most other nationals engaging in legal offshore financial activity. Granted, governmental authorities can make it difficult to migrate or invest offshore directly, but there are still legal and legitimate ways to do so.

Just recently *The Wall Street Journal* reported that "many wealthy individuals are turning to foreign entities, such as offshore trusts and insurance policies, as part of their tax planning and asset protection strategies. Although local citizens generally must report any foreign accounts and entities with their governments each year, going offshore could add extra roadblocks on an audit trail." We will look at some of these issues in this book.

You can expect local based lawyers, accountants, investment gurus, and insurance salesmen to do everything they can to discourage you from going to where the best investments and best asset protection reside – offshore. Naturally, they understand little beyond their local based clientele. And most of all, your friendly local tax agent wants nothing more than for you to keep your assets at home, so he can keep a close eye on your money.

One crucial difference for the citizens of the world to keep in mind: unlike almost all other nations, *the United States taxes all its citizens and permanent residents (green card holders) on their worldwide income* regardless of their place of residence or where the income is earned.

Virtually all nations, like the United Kingdom, Canada, Australia, and New Zealand exempt their citizens from taxes if they choose to live elsewhere.... but not the U.S.

So yes, it is perfectly legal for most of the western civilized world to move family and wealth outside of their homeland. And in most cases, even when you continue to live at home, you can legally open up an off-shore bank account for increased financial privacy and enhanced asset protection.

Plus, when going offshore you have the opportunity for increased investment protection and diversification from fluctuating currencies, since you have many currency choices rather than limiting yourself to your local currency. You can freely hold US Dollars, Euros, Swiss Francs, British Sterling, Japanese Yen, or Canadian, Australian or New Zealand Dollars, and most other currencies from around the world.

International investments make sense because they are in tune with the deepest aspects of reality. Nations and borders are illusions. Economics and human nature pass beyond these artificial barriers. We call our global actions free trade, but they are more. International invest-ments, global living and multinational trade are nature's expression of how people should be...human beings trading with one another, not Americans, Canadians, Chinese, Australians, British and so forth using past ideals to separate themselves.

Slowly, humanity is eliminating the false labels so we can live as we should, one person to another. Admittedly, we have a long way to go. At this stage of social evolution most political, educational and economic systems are out of tune with the real forces of human nature. They are slanted inwards by a variety of political forces that do not want its citi-zens to have a global view.

This is changing and will continue to change at a rapid pace. Technology and population growth are expressions of evolution. International investors can profit by helping finance this change.

If you're thinking of going offshore, you're not only "legally" in the right to hold assets offshore, you're a lot wiser individual if you take advantage of global opportunities. Your right to leave your homeland and emigrate to another is one of the most fundamental requirements of freedom..... and you don't need a law to give you that right!

Both the International Covenant on Civil and Political Rights (Art. 12) and the Universal Declaration of Human Rights (Art. 13(2)) confirm that emigration is a basic human right. But thanks to repressive tax policies followed by a growing number of countries around the world, this right is increasingly threatened.

Sad to say, contrary to popular delusions, the U.S. has long been the most egregious violator of the right of emigration. For more than 80 years, Congress has dictated that U.S. citizens are responsible for paying U.S. taxes, no matter where they live or where they earn.

Paying taxes on non-U.S. income by a non-U.S. residents living and working in a non-U.S. venue is fundamentally unfair. This is even more true when a U.S. citizen living abroad is also paying tax on his or her income in another country. And while many of these taxes should be credited against U.S. tax obligation, not all of them will, leading to double taxation. For example, the so-called foreign tax credits on U.S. tax returns are often lost by the alternative minimum tax calculations. And not to mention the additional cost of complying with two different sets of tax rules in the different jurisdictions.

Unfortunately, the only way that a U.S. citizen can legally escape the burden of paying U.S. taxes is to take the extreme measure of renouncing U.S. citizenship. And up until recently, if this act was considered "tax-motivated", the former U.S. citizen was responsible for paying U.S. tax on certain income for an additional 10 years and must submit to an invasive reporting regime during this period.... for better or for worse, we will explain how this area of law is developing.

What is frightening is that other world governments are following the lead of America's ability to literally tax its citizens to death, no matter where they live. The U.K., with Australia and Canada close behind, are following the U.S. lead in taxing its citizens from cradle to grave in virtually every segment of life.

One can't say that the handwriting isn't on the wall.

The solution to this aggressive tax expansion for some is to give up citizenship and acquire citizenship in a low or no tax country. As radical as this idea may seem at first glance, it's perfectly legal to give up citizenship as long as you have a good passport from another country. For those interested in renouncing citizenship, we will explore this topic in greater detail later. Keep in mind that this generally means first adopting another venue as your new homeland.

Physically relocating to another country presents some challenges, but most often they are surmountable. Long-term stays generally require visas or residency permits to new homelands. Each country has its own system and procedures to follow before making the move, and they are somewhat similar. Visas can sometimes be obtained while living in the new country, but often it is wisest to start the process before you relocate. We will explore how this process works by using New Zealand as an example to obtaining residency.

Arranging to sell or consolidate your existing home and belongings can be stressful. Looking for a new home or work, if not retired or self-employed, can be even more daunting. And trying to understand the local cultural ways, language and mannerisms present yet another fresh set of challenges as you attempt to assimilate your host country's ways.

Is it all worth it? For the majority of people willing to keep an open mind, the answer is an astonishing yes.

However, frequently overlooked during the process of an international move are legal and tax pre-planning issues. Too often, I have seen expats give no advance attention to these essential matters and wait until *after* they are settled into their adopted country. The problems that arise by failing to take proper steps in advance to legally minimize your taxes, for example, can be an expensive and time-consuming nightmare.

For American citizens and tax residents, the tax gauntlet is the worst of all, since they pay taxes on worldwide income regardless of where they live, where the money is earned, and whether or not it is passive or earned income. American citizens have the harshest, most difficult and most confusing set of tax laws worldwide.... but there is *some* relief, and we also explore those ideas throughout this book.

The good news: with a little forethought you can minimize your legal issues and tax burdens, and make life easier. As we proceed through the book, we will look at the above and many other benefits of going off-shore, and how to make the transition smoother.

Stop and think for just a few moments about the endlessly changing world around you and what this means for the future. When we are blinded by our ignorance about changes taking place, we fail to act at our own peril. Here are some of my favorite excerpts from *"The Experts Speak: The Definitive Compendium of Authoritative Misinformation"* by Christopher Cerf and Victor S. Navasky:

What can be more palpably absurd than the prospect held out of loco-motives traveling twice as fast as stagecoaches?

The Quarterly Review, England (March 1825)

The abolishment of pain in surgery is a chimera. It is absurd to go on seeking it. Knife and pain are two words in surgery that must forever be associated in the consciousness of the patient.

Dr Alfred Velpeau (1839) French surgeon

Men might as well project a voyage to the Moon as attempt to employ steam navigation against the stormy North Atlantic Ocean.

Dr Dionysus Lardner (1838) Professor of Natural Philosophy and Astronomy, University College, London

[W]hen the Paris Exhibition closes electric light will close with it and no more be heard of.

Erasmus Wilson (1878) Professor at Oxford University

Well-informed people know it is impossible to transmit the voice over wires and that were it possible to do so, the thing would be of no prac-tical value.

Editorial in the Boston Post (1865)

That the automobile has practically reached the limit of its development is suggested by the fact that during the past year no improvements of a radical nature have been introduced.

> *Scientific American, Jan. 2, 1909*

Heavier-than-air flying machines are impossible.

> *Lord Kelvin, ca. 1895, British mathematician and physicist*

Radio has no future

> *Lord Kelvin, ca. 1897*

There is not the slightest indication that nuclear energy will ever be obtainable. It would mean that the atom would have to be shattered at will.

> *Albert Einstein, 1932.*

There is no need for any individual to have a computer in their home.

> *Ken Olson, 1977, President Digital Equipment Corp.*

Stocks have reached a permanently high plateau.

> *Irving Fisher; Professor of Economics at Yale University, October 17, 1929*

We don't like their sound..... groups of guitars are on their way out.

> *Decca Recording Company executive, turning down the Beatles, 1962*

I think there is a world market for maybe five computers.

> *Thomas Watson, chairman of IBM, 1943.*

Over the long run, nations and borders are illusions, and social and political change is inevitable. It is important to recognize the changes happening before us so we can learn to adapt.

CHAPTER TWO

Border Controls

A significant change occurring globally are increased restrictions and controls placed upon persons and properties when crossing borders. Simple, easy passage across political boundaries is a throw back to recent history as the future looks bleak.

If you think it's bad enough to unpack and reload your laptop during airport inspections, the actual contents have also become subject to inspection upon entering the United States. That's right, a recent and controversial decision by the 9th Circuit Court of Appeals in California held that the U.S. Customs Officials may seize and search travelers' laptops upon entering the U.S. even in the absence of search warrant or probable cause.

The traditional 4th Amendment protection offered by the U.S. Constitution does not apply to airport searches, held this Court. *"The government may conduct routine searches of persons entering the United States without probable cause, reasonable suspicion, or a warrant,"* the court stated, citing the U.S. Supreme Court's 1985 ruling in <u>United States v. Montoya de Hernandez</u>, 473 U.S. 531."

There is one glimmer of hope to this expanded intrusion against our right to free travel. A U.S. district judge in California recently issued a contradictory ruling on this issue, concluding that Customs has to have "reasonable suspicion" of wrongdoing in order to search your laptop. That's still a lower burden of causality than "probable cause", which is typical under a criminal law standard.

The "reasonable suspicion" standard is now required in Los Angeles before Customs agents can conduct a body cavity search, X-rays, or other invasive examinations.... so if you're crossing the border anywhere else, Customs officials can presumably still conduct a search for any reason they desire. I suspect that the matter won't be resolved until competing appeals reach the U.S. Supreme Court in a few years.

And there is more.

If the U.S. government gets its way, beginning soon we'll all be on "no-fly" lists, unless and until the government gives us permission to leave or re-enter the United States. The U.S. Department of Homeland Security (DHS) has proposed that all airlines, cruise lines, even fishing boats, be required to obtain clearance for each passenger they propose taking into or out of the United States.

It doesn't matter if you have a U.S. passport "travel document" which currently, absent a court order to the contrary, grants you virtually an unqualified right to enter or leave the United States, any time you want. If the new DHS system comes into effect as requested, and the agency says "no" to a clearance request, *or doesn't answer the request at all,* you won't be permitted to enter or leave the United States.

By way of example, consider what might happen to even a U.S. passport holder living or working outside of the U.S. Your visa is about to expire, so you board your flight back to the United States. But wait! You can't get on, because you don't have permission from the DHS. Your host country immigration officials are on hand to escort you to a squalid detention center, where you and others who are now effectively "stateless persons" are detained indefinitely, until your immigration status is sorted out.

Why might the DHS deny you permission to leave or enter the United States? No one knows, because the entire clearance procedure would be a secretive administrative determination, with no right of appeal. Naturally, the decision would be made without a warrant, without probable cause and without even any particular degree of suspicion. Basically, if the DHS decides it doesn't like you, or fails to promptly respond, you're a prisoner either outside, or inside, the United States, whether or not you hold a U.S. passport.

If the U.S. treats it own passport holders as above, what type of treatment do you think this means for foreign travelers?

The U.S. Supreme Court has long recognized there is a constitutional right to travel internationally. Indeed, it has declared that the right to travel is "a virtually unconditional personal right." The United States has also signed treaties guaranteeing "freedom of travel." So if these regulations do go into effect, you can expect a lengthy court battle, both nationally and internationally.

Think this can't happen? Think again...it's *already* happening. Earlier this year, DHS forbade airlines from transporting an 18-year-old native-born U.S. citizen, back to the United States. The prohibition lasted nearly six months until it was finally lifted.

And on the Canadian frontier, freedom of passage is becoming an oxymoron.

We all know the War on Terror hasn't snagged very many terrorists. However, at the Canadian border thousands of innocent tourists are denied entry because of relatively minor offenses they faced decades ago.

Did you inhale during the 1960s and get caught? If you were convicted for even misdemeanor possession of marijuana Canada's borders are closed off to you. What's more, any criminal offense you committed as an adult is now part of a vast database shared with Canadian immigration authorities.

Even convictions for trespassing, public intoxication and shoplifting will forbid you from crossing the border. While you may think those youthful indiscretions were trivial and long forgotten, the computer has not.

These sweeping cross-border restrictions into Canada are part of a new information-exchange agreement first started between the United States and Canada after 9/11. Importantly, other countries are beginning to tap into the "Smart Border Action Plan" and you can count on more of this type of infringement to freedom of travel in the near future.

The U.S.-Canadian model is also used with all other countries under the "visa waiver" agreements with the United States. These programs provide immigration officials in countries around the world to access U.S. arrest and conviction data complied by the Department of Homeland Security database, and gives U.S. officials access to comparable data in Canada.

Nazi Germany and the Soviet Union are two countries in recent history that didn't allow their citizens to travel abroad without permission. If these regulations go into effect, you can add the United States to this list.

It is depressing to watch America, Australia, Canada and the European countries take the long march down the road assaulting natural rights and freedoms, saying nothing to established international laws. As these impediments to the free and natural movement of people and property worsen, being able to manage risk across political boundaries becomes increasingly important. Offshore risk management becomes essential for those looking beyond the horizons.

CHAPTER THREE

Offshore Risk Management

For those who are concerned about "going offshore" for asset protection, investment diversification or doing business, it may be helpful to remember that risk is always relative. Jumping out of a second story window is certainly high on the risk scale, but if the building is on fire and you can't get out any other way, the two-story jump is a lot less risky than staying where you are.

Let's first look at some of the reasons why an increasing number of people in the U.S., Canada and Australia are diversifying some of their assets offshore.

There is an ongoing hot debate, especially in America, between those who believe there is 'no place like home' and those who believe their homeland is increasingly becoming a police state in which our traditional liberties are being circumvented by a host of draconian laws.

On the one hand, the western cultures, particularly the USA, do offer many economic and personal benefits not readily available around the world. The U.S. does have the largest economy in the world with freedom to choose career paths and work towards economic independence. There is great freedom of movement *within* the American, Canadian or Australian borders, and there is not a burden of multiplicity of languages as exists in Europe. And for the most part, it is still possible to write and publish information critical of the government and its policies.

Notwithstanding, there is a growing cancer in the body politics of these countries, lead by the American government, that many fear are irreversible. First was the 'war on drugs' that led to the creation of a curious felony known as money laundering. While this law was created on the pretext that it would hurt the drug dealers, it became a huge trap for innocent people diversifying assets who have no ties to any form of criminal activity.

Another casualty to our natural rights and freedoms is the right to be secure in the possession of our property, which is supposedly protected by the Fourth Amendment to the U.S. Constitution. Nearly any government agent or police officer can accuse you of a crime and then proceed to confiscate your property even if it is only remotely connected to the alleged crime. Abuses of asset forfeiture laws are becoming legendary. In many federal agencies, states, counties and cities, revenues from forfeitures have become a substitute for allotted funds to pay for the law enforcement activities. As a result, law enforcement personnel are left to their own devices to create opportunities for forfeitures to meet their budgets.

With no pride, I report that the U.S. now has more people in prison per 1,000 citizens than any other country in the world. You might be surprised to know that a high percentage of the prison inmates generally were not involved in harm to others, their property, or any kind of theft or fraud. The so-called crimes are a result of behavior inconsistent with politically accepted norms. With the overwhelming and growing number of Federal, State, County, local and municipal laws and regulations, it has reached a point in America where it is virtually impossible to be totally innocent of every kind of crime because of the overly complex rules and laws at every level of government.

Americans who are financially successful are not safe or secure in their possessions for many reasons – including a burdensome level of taxation on the well-to-do. And Canadians, Australians and Europeans cannot take relief since they are traveling down the same path.

In America, the top 10% of the income earners pay more than 50% of the total individual income tax. The bottom 50% pays virtually no income taxes. The U.S., like its brethren in the other western countries, increasingly penalizes those that earn and save. In spite of increasing social entitlements to the underachievers, the mass media and many politicians continue to rally against the high producers and earners, denying them the benefits of what they have produced and saved.

Another concern for all of western civilization is the risk of currency controls. Historically, this has always been an issue, and presently exists today in varying degrees in many countries. Yes, even the U.S., Canada, Australia or Europe could establish currency controls and prohibit citizens from taking any assets out of the country.... there is an abundance of history that teaches this hard lesson.

We are only left to speculate on the provisions of any future laws on currency controls that may be imposed in the U.S. or other western countries. However, without sounding too "professorial" on the topic, we can only look to history as an example and as a guide of what *could* happen to our savings.

For example, Nazi Germany, South Africa and Russia are all the best (or worse) examples of recent currency controls restricting citizens from leaving the country with local currency. I personally have friends from South Africa who are honest, hard working business people that resettled in New Zealand and Australia and have shared their personal stories with me of their nightmares when they tried to expatriate their assets outside of their country with currency controls .... depressing tales indeed.

And too, I have a long time friend who was a well-know actress married to a famous composer from Russia that shared their story as they tried to leave their country with their hard-earned wealth. Sad to say, I had a friend that committed suicide over the prospect of losing everything and the fear of starting over again in his late 50s.

The above examples of currency controls are as recent as only the 1990s. But even today in China – the global economic steam engine – its citizens and foreign investors looking to move money offshore are hindered by strict currency prohibitions. The government holds a heavy hand over foreign exchange mechanisms and exchange rate controls. The amount of Chinese Renmimbi Yuan that leaves the country is severely limited.

What's more, we have all heard the horror stories from the 1930s and 1940s as people fled Germany and Eastern Europe with what little they had as they desperately tried to save themselves from tyrants. So the bottom line is that as a good student of history I take the issue of currency controls very seriously and as a realistic event that could occur anywhere, at any time, including in the U.S. Having at least a portion of your assets offshore is a good starting point for risk management.

In each of the above examples, those folks that had pre-planning strategies and held their assets titled in a foreign structure (an international trust is an excellent risk management tool) and located in a foreign country did not have the concerns of the average person who did not. If history is our teacher, and if we learn well, I can see no better way to protect assets than titling them in an offshore international trust structure and holding them outside of a home country.

If you suddenly desired or needed to move assets across borders and were prohibited, who would pay for your care? Those with money are always more welcome in a host country than the indigent. Even if you don't have a good reason to leave your homeland today, there is always peace of mind in knowing that you can, if it ever becomes necessary.

But there are other reasons and benefits in having some assets located offshore. While there might be plenty of investment opportunities within your country, they are not necessarily the best for every investor. There are an overwhelming number of choices available outside your backyard, just "offshore."

Putting all of your eggs in one basket potentially poses great risk for those who fail to actively devote their time to managing their investment portfolio. The solution is diversification, another example of risk management.

Diversification is simply an organized system of managing and mitigating various types and levels of risks. The main investment risk is often not being able to cash in your investments at full value when you need them. This risk is often minimized or avoided by investing in low yield and liquid forms of savings like certificates of deposits, term deposits, T-Bills, Money Market Funds, and certain short-term corporate and government securities.

However, even those investments are subject to a loss of purchasing power due to inflation and the income they produce is heavily taxed. While common stocks, real estate and natural resource investments sometimes provide a better hedge against inflation and even some tax deferral, they are subject to risk of illiquidity and a deflationary economy.

There are many other types of risk that fall under liquidity risk, that is, a risk associated with not being able to gain immediate access to your money or obtain its reasonable value. Therefore, a diversified investment portfolio should include a broad band of assets, in different countries, and best yet, in different currencies. While you might be able to create a diversified investment portfolio in different currencies through your local bank, having investments outside a single political jurisdiction is a far superior form of asset diversification from risks associated at home.

And yes, contrary to what your local broker tells you, there are an overwhelming number of investment opportunities away from home. If you have an interest in doing business or reaching out to an enhanced number of investment opportunities, this may be all you need to know to go "offshore."

Do you think that depositing your savings in your hometown bank is safer than "offshore"? Think again.

Insurance involves a fund of assets that are based on the statistical likelihood that some risk event will occur in the future. To offset that risk, premiums are paid by policyholders based on the average potential claim or loss to some of the policyholders. For example, if one out of 100 policyholders is likely to incur a loss of $50,000, then each of the policyholders would have to pay a share to cover that loss. Rest assured, insurance companies are in the business of making money and don't intentionally insure people who are likely to have a claim. If your home is located in a high-risk fire or flood zone, private insurance is not possible, unless it's issued by the government.

The free savings and checking insurance and preferences for patriots are neither free nor insured. In the U.S. this is known as the Federal Deposit Insurance Corporation (FDIC).

With so called "government insurance", there is no statistical analysis on potential claims. Instead, when a claim arises, it's simply paid from your government's general funds, i.e. from your tax dollars. Government insurance is not based on any calculated or rational analysis of paid-in premiums to offset losses.

Unfortunately, this government-subsidized insurance encourages banks and savings and loans to be more aggressive than they would be if it was their money standing behind a pool of claims. S & Ls and banks compete with each other to offer the cheapest car or mortgage loan and the highest deposit rates. This results in a lack of discipline and fiscal conservatism in banking functions operating with your money. The government protective programs for patriots encourage riskier investing.

This example became obvious during the U.S. S & L crisis during the 1980s. And only a few years ago, some S & L managers, forgetting the hard lessons learned only a decade earlier, were investing depositors monies in high risk 'junk bonds', speculative derivatives and option investments.

Surprising to most Americans is the fact that many of the major international banks and insurance companies operating offshore are far more conservative in managing their portfolios and far less susceptible to failure than U.S. financial institutions. Many banks located "offshore" are highly rated investment quality at AA and AA-, a rating that even many of the best U.S. banks could never achieve.

Why are U.S. banks rated lower that many offshore banks?

Because offshore banks are generally not propped up by government-backed insurance to protect their depositors and must conduct their affairs with fiscal responsibility.

By comparison, U.S. banks and financial institutions are far more leveraged than many offshore financial institutions as a result of the government backed insurance programs. If the U.S. suffered a run against deposits – as happened in the 1930s – there would be great risk to the entire banking system, which could cause the entire system to fail. It is true that while depositors may be protected in the event of a few isolated failures, there is much greater portfolio risk in covering losses in a highly leveraged banking system such as the U.S., if all of your eggs are deposited into one banking system. Prudent and conservative U.S. investors therefore place some funds outside the U.S. banking system.... and the same is true for all nationals.

Another reason for moving part of your cash offshore is the loss of financial privacy. Increasingly, we have become a transparent society, and this includes our financial affairs. If you wish to know about someone else's financial situation, what they own, how much and where, for little more than a few dollars on the Internet you can obtain a wealth of information about anyone who interests you. And the reverse is also true. Your financial privacy is an open book to anyone who really bothers to find out.

What's more, state and federal governments regularly monitor mobile phone transmissions, email, wire transfers and other electronic communications looking for a pattern of messages that might suggest there is some drug, criminal or terrorist activity. Don't think for a minute that the professional criminals aren't aware of this and take aggressive steps to keep secret what concerns them most. Unfortunately, it is the innocent and unsuspecting individual who gets investigated because of some innocent comments made electronically. And didn't I previously mention how government agencies and the police force in the U.S. use and abuse asset seizure laws to fund their operating budgets?

What's more, I personally believe that one of the major reasons for placing some funds outside of your home country is due to the ongoing litigation epidemic. This first started in the U.S., most notably during the 1980s, worsened during the 1990s, and continues to grower bleaker every year. I wrote at length about the U.S. litigation problem and the need to seek offshore asset protection in *How to Legally Protect Your Assets*. The book grew out of years of litigation experience where I witnessed first hand asset protection plans that worked, and others that failed.

A significant reason for the flight of large amounts of assets moving offshore is the growing, crazy, litigious attitude and obnoxious awards granted by juries and judges. The U.S. is the only country in the world that permits lawyers to work on a contingent fee basis and to collect huge fees from punitive damage awards. As a former U.S. litigation attorney myself, and a former judge, I can attest to the ridiculous claims and results that too frequently arise from the U.S. judicial system. It is broken, and I see little hope or opportunity to fix it while the present system exists.

It is well-known that the U.S. courts and juries have become the most generous in the world in awarding damages to plaintiffs. The judges and the juries are often sympathetic to the claims of the plaintiff and look for someone to pay for the damages. And even insurance has limited benefits, since the insurance companies often badger their insured to settle to avoid a trial.... even with the most frivolous of lawsuits. This is well-known to plaintiff lawyers and only serves to encourage them and their clients to seek never-ending creative ways to sue anyone with any assets, particularly when covered by insurance.

Not to be left far behind, the litigation prospects for Canada, Australia and Europe aren't too much better. While these countries aren't nearly as bad as the U.S., regrettably they are not far behind in developing the same mentality of the U.S. where a claimant seeks to find blame against someone else for their circumstances. Living in New Zealand and spending considerable time in Australia over recent years, I see the same themes developing there today that I first witnessed in the U.S. during the 1980s and 1990s. Sad, indeed.

What most people fail to recognize is that every new law which confers a right also imposes a duty on someone else to subsidize that right. An excellent discussion of the growth of laws in the U.S. is covered in *The Death of Common Sense,* by Philip K. Howard. While you read almost daily of new laws being passed to guarantee some right for a perceived wrong, when is the last time you read about a law that was written off the books?

Our country has become a financially cannibalistic society where we compete in the legal and political arenas for the power to impose our wills and policies on others. Those who mind their own business, put their nose to the grindstone and are thrifty, too often find themselves unsuspectedly on the short end of the deal. The hard-working individuals in our culture who have accumulated some assets or who have become financially independent, need to set aside at least a small nest-egg offshore, where it will be safe from the litigation parasites and politically-connected vultures in our society.

To be forewarned is to be forearmed.

The case for using an international trust for risk management is stronger today than ever before. While the topic of an international trust is covered later in this book, I provide much more detail and useful examples of this asset protection planning tool in *How to Legally Protect Your Assets.*

So yes again, going offshore is perfectly legal. As the barriers at the borders continue to become increasingly restrictive against the free movement of people and property, going offshore provides an opportunity to broaden your horizons and better manage risks.

What do you need to know before taking your next step of living or investing offshore? In the next few chapters we look at some of the fundamental principles and legal issues of moving people across international borders.

OFFSHORE AND MORE

As I grow older, I pay less attention to what men say.
I just watch what they do.
Andrew Carnegie

CHAPTER FOUR

Moving Offshore – Residency, Citizenship & Domicile

Here is the skinny on what you need to know before moving yourself offshore..... and then some.

First, understand there is a difference between domicile, residency and citizenship..... all with important legal and tax ramifications. A book could be written on the topic – and probably has – but here is a very brief summary.

Domicile is where you call home and live. Even with multiple places of abode, with equal time spent between them, only one will be called your domicile. Domicile can be determined "as a matter of fact", or as a "legal fiction." Your domicile gives rise to many legal issues, like rights upon divorce, death, inheritances, and more.... but they are beyond this discussion.

Residency has basically two faces. Legal residency and tax residency.

Legal residency gives you a right to reside or spend time in a place or country. You can have legal residency in one or more country at the same time. When you travel as a visitor or tourist to another country, depending where you are going, you are granted a Visa or right to reside or visit that destination temporarily. Many countries have already negotiated on your behalf, for Visa free travel to other countries, so actual written or advance travel permission is not required.

Those countries where Visa free travel has not been negotiated by treaty require you to make a Visa application in advance for permission to come across the political boundaries for a permitted duration of stay. Depending on your purpose, i.e. business or tourism, the Visa can vary in length. These Visas are generally one to three months in length, but under special business or working classifications, I have seen them as long as one or two years.

Legal residency can also be obtained for longer durations of stay, for purposes of living in a country. A country looking to acquire a class of immigrants sets a standard or criteria for interested immigrants to migrate. For example, a typical situation would be a shortage of skilled workers in a growing country looking to attract people with those skills and the entry requirements for those immigrants are reduced... e.g. New Zealand.

And too, a common classification is a business or investor category Visa where the investor agrees to invest certain amounts of money for a minimum amount of time into a certain category of investments in the host country. Retired persons can have an advantage in one country looking to attract these types of immigrants, or be a detriment in another country which is looking for younger, skilled workers that can contribute to their country. There are other classifications, and the entry requirements change – sometimes frequently – as targets are reached and new government goals are obtained.

Frequently with legal residency, you obtain permission to stay for a set term. For example, you could be granted a three-year temporary residency to live in a country. Then, so long as you have been a good guest in the host country (i.e. stay out of legal problems and satisfy the residency requirements), after the three-year term you would typically obtain permanent or indefinite residency. You can then stay forever if you like. Naturally, you are free to come and go. Just think of the temporary residency as a "courtship" for you and your host country to get to know each other more intimately.

Then there is tax residency.

Tax residency is an entirely different animal from legal residency and one is not necessarily dependent upon the other. Tax residency is generally defined as being acquired if you live within a country for a term which is more than a set number of days. Thereafter you become obligated to pay income taxes to the host country. It is very common for countries to declare you a tax resident if you live 183 days in a calendar or running year. So if you are in the country legally or illegally, on a short or long term permanent Visa (legal residency), regardless of whether you are a citizen or not, you become obliged to pay a percentage of your income to your adopted country in the name of taxes.

Tax residency becomes a very complex issue as you have probably guessed. In most countries around the world, you would not be obligated to pay taxes unless you actually live in the country or earn income in the country for a set period of time. And too, even if you are a tax resident you can move in and then out of the country and no longer be considered a tax resident after a certain duration and be tax free from the former country.... but if you are a U.S. citizen, disregard this opportunity.

Unfortunately, the USA is not one of those countries where mobility and changing tax status is such a freedom.

Tax residency income tax obligations are designed to be lessened by certain tax provisions or through bi-lateral and multi-lateral tax treaties that countries enter into together to allow "tax free mobility" of their working citizens abroad. Unfortunately, this term is often no more than an oxymoron, and the full benefit can be difficult to achieve at times.

Living in another country doesn't require citizenship, only a Visa for a short or long term residency in that country. Moreover, Visa requirements vary from country to country – it's always a moving target – but obtaining a Visa is the easiest way to move and live "offshore", wherever that might be. For example, in just one year New Zealand changed its pass mark requirements for obtaining a Visa 5 or 6 times, going from relatively easy to very difficult. As new immigration targets were made, and objectives reached, the pass marks changed.

If you are thinking of moving to New Zealand, for example, there is a section later in the book that covers the process. But in general, don't wait to apply for long-term residency if you are age 50 or over. Deductions to pass marks start to occur once you hit 50 (e.g. in NZ & AU) and it becomes very difficult to obtain residency after age 54. The reason is that New Zealand is looking for young and skilled labor to migrate into the country. The exception is for those that have a bucket load of money to invest or are interested in establishing a new business enterprise that creates jobs and opportunities.

On the other hand, certain countries cater to retirees with a minimum amount of money to support themselves (e.g. certain Caribbean Islands and Central American countries), or to the very wealthy (Switzerland, Singapore, Hong Kong & even Ireland). This is important if you desire to obtain a Visa or eventually a second passport in the host country you are looking to move.

Keep in mind that residency or citizenship in one country does not mean a right to live in another country. For example, Italian citizenship (or any other EU citizenship) will not provide long-term residency in Canada or even most other non-EU countries, any more than U.S. citizenship will provide you with that right. There are certain EU exceptions, but even an EU Passport does not necessarily open the doors for permanent residency in all other EU jurisdictions.

Most importantly, start with where you wish to live and see how your objective of living there can be accomplished.

For a close friend of mine, obtaining Italian citizenship was a long, long road, since she had to carve out new territory with a very narrowly defined Italian law that apparently had been passed years earlier for a wealthy person with political clout trying to gain citizenship in Italy.... at least that is my take on it. It was mere co-incidence that she discovered the law and creatively fitted herself into a very narrowly defined set of circumstances, and she had to practically threaten litigation with an Italian Consulates Office to force them to apply the law to her circumstances.... but it worked.

Can you too obtain new citizenship in a new country?

In general, countries define citizenship based on one's descent, place of birth, marriage, and/or naturalization. That is, you might have a right to citizenship with a new country based upon one or more of the following reasons:

- You were born on territory belonging to, or claimed by, that country (often called *ius soli,* or sometimes *jus soli* – Latin for "right of the soil").

- One or both of your parents were citizens of that country (often called *ius sanguinis* or *jus sanguinis* – Latin for "right of the blood").

- You married a citizen of that country (though please note that the practice of granting immediate, automatic citizenship to a foreign spouse is far less prevalent today than it was decades ago).

- You (or one or both of your parents) obtained that country's citizenship by going through a legal process of *naturalization.*

So there are various routes to obtaining a new citizenship.

No one knows for sure how many Americans are also citizens of other lands, because neither the U.S. nor other governments keep track. Estimates range from 500,000 to 5.7 million people.

International attitudes toward dual citizenship vary. Some nations forbid it. Some encourage it. Most – like the United States – officially deplore it, but tolerate it. In all, 93 nations permit dual citizenship in one form or another.

About 40 million Americans are eligible for dual citizenship in another country, usually because of family ties. Legally, dual citizenship for U.S. citizens is clearly available. This right occurred in 1967 when the U.S. Supreme Court struck down U.S. laws forbidding dual citizenship. It has gained momentum over the past decade as other countries have changed their laws to allow citizens, former citizens, their children and even grandchildren and great grandchildren to carry more than one passport.

The official U.S. position on dual citizenship reads in part: The U.S. Government recognizes that dual nationality exists but does not encourage it as a matter of policy because of the "problems" it may cause. For example, it is argued, the U.S. government may not be able to assist you as readily if you are a dual citizen since there are multiple legal rights associated with another country's citizenship. However, in my humble opinion, the real concern is the risk these people have in losing their connection with the U.S. is the lost revenue base from tax generating citizens kept under tight scrutiny closer at home.

The official Canadian position on dual citizenship is that the Citizenship Act allows a Canadian citizen to acquire foreign nationality without automatically losing Canadian citizenship. Since February 15, 1977, a Canadian citizen may retain Canadian citizenship, unless he or she voluntarily applies to renounce it and the application is approved by a citizenship judge. The present Act thus makes it possible to have two or more citizenships and allegiances at the same time for an indefinite period.

Also, both the U.S. and Canada require specific acts to give up citizenship. Canada requires that someone who wants to give up their Canadian citizenship has to go to a Canadian embassy or consulate and sign a special form in the presence of Canadian officials. The U.S.

requires that "A person wishing to renounce his or her U.S. citizenship must voluntarily and with intent to relinquish U.S. citizenship appear in person before a U.S. consular or diplomatic officer, in a foreign country (normally at a U.S. Embassy or Consulate), and sign an oath of renunciation. Also required today are certain tax forms to be completed to disclose assets before renouncing U.S. citizenship.

While I wasn't able to obtain Australia's "official" position on Aussies obtaining dual citizenship, I did locate a page on a government web site that specifically gave guidance on how its citizens could obtain U.S. and other dual citizenships. I don't believe this is because the Australian government is trying to encourage dual citizenship, but because they probably received so many questions on the topic they decided to post the information online for its citizens.

Note that the respective governments often couch dual citizenship in negative terms as few governments like to lose control over their citizens.

For those readers who are interested in rights of dual citizenship associated with U.S. citizenship, the historical development of the right, and where it might lead us next, I have included a section on the topic later in the book.

Which Countries today *allow* dual citizenship? Bangladesh, Brazil, Canada, Colombia, Cyprus, Egypt, El Salvador, Federal Republic of Yugoslavia, France, Greece, Hungary, Ireland, Israel, Italy, Jordan, Latvia, Lebanon, Lithuania, Macedonia, Malta, Mexico, New Zealand, Pakistan*, Portugal, Serbia and Montenegro, South Africa*, Spain (only in certain cases), Sweden, Switzerland, Syria, Tonga (only in certain cases), Turkey, United Kingdom, United States of America, Western Samoa. (* Persons retain their former citizenship if they apply to retain it before taking out citizenship.)

Countries which *prohibit* dual citizenship: Austria, Belgium, Brunei, Burma, Chile, China, Denmark, Ecuador, Fiji, Finland, Germany*, Iceland, India*, Indonesia, Iran*, Japan, Kenya, Kiribati, Korea, Malaysia, Mauritius, Nepal, Norway, Papua New Guinea, Peru, Philippines, Poland, Romania, Singapore, Solomon Islands, Thailand, Venezuela, Vietnam, Zimbabwe. (*Iran does not recognize dual citizenship but continues to recognize its citizens as Iranian. *Note that

Germany has recently amended its citizenship laws so that in some exceptional circumstances, dual citizenship is now allowed. Consult the German Foreign Office for details. *Also, India announced recently that it will change its law to allow dual citizenship for Indians settled outside India.)

And if you do obtain dual citizenship, with U.S. being one of your citizenships, then keep in mind that U.S. Federal Law requires, in general, that any U.S. citizen who is either leaving or entering the U.S. must be in possession of a valid U.S. passport. This requirement applies even in the case of a dual citizen traveling between the U.S. and their other country of citizenship. A person in such a situation may therefore need to take two passports for the trip – one from the US, and one from the other country.

Certain exceptions to the U.S. passport requirement are spelled out in Section 53 of Title 22 of the *Code of Federal Regulations*. Even though the title of this section suggests that it is applicable only in time of war or national emergency, in fact it applies at all times. In addition, a U.S. passport is now required, for example, when traveling between the US and adjacent countries in the Western Hemisphere, such as Canada or Mexico.

Another exception to the U.S. passport requirement exists for young children with dual U.S./other citizenship. A dual-citizen child under age 12 may travel without a U.S. passport if he or she is listed as a dependent in the foreign passport of an alien parent. In such a situation, other evidence of the child's U.S. citizenship (such as a birth certificate) will have to be shown when returning to the U.S. Note, however, that this exception may be of limited usefulness if the airline being used chooses not to honor it. For example, I have personally seen situations where an airline refused to allow a U.S.-born child of foreign decent parent-citizens to board a U.S.-bound flight unless the child also had a valid U.S. passport.

The U.S. does not currently have official "exit controls" at its borders, but this too is evolving as noted earlier. Needing to obtain DHS prior "permission" to enter or depart would constitute an exit control rule for all practical purposes, as far as I am concerned.

If your objective is to simply give up citizenship to stop paying taxes, that presents an entirely new and complicated set of issues. For example, in the U.S. there are specific U.S. tax laws enacted over recent years to discourage (read prevent) U.S. citizens from expatriating for tax reasons. Previously, if your assets and/or income were over a certain level you could continue to pay income taxes on certain income into the future, but this too is evolving as covered later. Suffice it to say this is an entirely new, complicated issue that may affect you, depending on assets and income....... but advance planning to work around the issues can help make this objective easier to overcome.

Once you make a move to a new country you have to consider the implications of paying taxes in your adopted homeland. When living in another country there are bilateral tax treaties to supposedly prevent you from paying double taxes on the same income, but as pointed out elsewhere, I have found this doesn't always work out as the treaties are written. For example, the U.S. tax code and AMT (that dirty thing called alternative minimum tax) is a royal pain in the back side, and foreign tax credits can disappear, ending up with an obligation to pay taxes to two different countries on the same income.... not a pleasant result.

What is supposed to occur is a U.S. taxpayer receives foreign tax credit for taxes paid to one country against tax obligations due to the other country. With careful planning it can and does work, but with limitations: 1) You will generally need to work with two accountants (one in each country) and 2) U.S. citizens need to be aware that the AMT can result in lost foreign tax credits causing double taxation.

Is there a way for expatriating citizens to avoid the double tax problem? Yes, with proper pre-migration planning this can often be accomplished. However, too often I have seen expats completely ignore this aspect, get hammered with double taxation, and some even returning to their home jurisdiction in frustration over the dual tax systems. (Hint..... the best plan is to avoid this problem is generally with a pre-migration type trust, also covered later).

So, acquiring a new citizenship to move to Canada or New Zealand to avoid taxes, particularly for U.S. citizens due to worldwide taxation, may not be a sustainable plan. An aggressive U.S. tax minimization program would probably be much easier, quicker and cheaper, if your goal is primarily to reduce your U.S. taxes.

If your goal is to begin anew a different life or invest outside of your home country, are there better options? You bet.

However, it does take some forethought to decide what you want to accomplish, spend some time to do your homework, make a plan, and then make the commitment to make it work. It is definitely worthwhile. Our family has thrived upon the new experiences and our children have opened their eyes to a whole new world beyond the narrow perspectives of where they began. I am proud to say our two daughters are truly citizens of the world.

I don't want to overwhelm you with details, but if some 200,000 Americans per year emigrate from the U.S. alone, so can you. The world population today is indeed increasingly mobile, notwithstanding new draconian laws to hinder the free movement of people and property.

So there you have it in a nutshell.

There is a spot waiting for you on the beach if you are committed to starting a new and exciting life. Might your lifestyle be enhanced with dual citizenship and a second passport.... the next topic we explore.

CHAPTER FIVE

Dual Citizenship and a Second Passport

As you might imagine, the pages of my passports are filled with official Customs and Immigration stamps from many nations. I have on more than one occasion been told that there was no space left to place a stamp and that I "must" obtain a new passport.

I have offices both inside and outside of the U.S., and travel thousands of miles each year back and forth to the U.S., Europe, Asia, the South Pacific, and Latin America. Occasionally I run into an over-zealous customs officer who examines my well-traveled passport and sneers: "You travel an awful lot - why?" Fixing his eyes with mine, I reply in my best courtroom voice: "Because, I'm an International Lawyer." "Oh!" is the response, and my passport is quickly stamped, and I am waived on. No need to tangle with an International Lawyer, he reasons. Touché!

Unfortunate, however, is how frequently travelers today have to put up with the nonsensical, arrogant display of unquestioned authority which government border control agents display. Ambassadors of goodwill welcoming you into their country they are not. Instead, in this brave new world, everyone is treated as a criminal.

Today, American travelers flying to even nearby locations across the border need passports. Until recently, a motor vehicle operator's license or other photo ID has been sufficient. As of January 2007, U.S. citizens leaving or entering the country from airports in Canada, Bermuda, Mexico, Panama and South and Central America were required to present valid U.S. passports in order to be allowed back into the United States. Land and sea travel will be included as of January 2008.

According to Washington, this is a security measure recommended by the 9/11 Commission. However it is unclear to me exactly how this added inconvenience will bar terrorists. Some of the 9/11 hijackers used falsified passports to enter the country, and others had valid U.S. Visas. Someone determined to do wrong will find a way notwithstanding the burden placed on the rest of us.

These new measures are just one more example of the Orwellian prophecy as Big Brother continues to find ways to keeps tabs on what we are doing.

Continually, the use of passports is a government means of coercion against its citizens. In the U.S. a citizen can be denied a passport simply for being in debt to the Internal Revenue Service, because of other problems with federal government agencies or simply because they are behind in even small amounts for court ordered child support.

Moreover, the U.S. State Department informs the IRS of all persons who renew their U.S. passports using a foreign address. Why is this necessary? Since passport renewals also require an applicant's Social Security number, this is used by the IRS to see if applicants have filed income tax returns.

Even worse, there are other personal threats arising from your government. Depending on your nation's policies, your government may use your passport to restrict your basic human right to travel, rather than to guarantee it. Use of your passport can be made contingent on payment of your taxes, even when disputed. Issuance of your passport allows your government to control, restrict, monitor, and record your travels.

What is even more distressing is that there is a growing tendency in other western countries to follow the unfortunate lead of the United States.

Alternative citizenship is, therefore, increasingly important as a powerful tool for international travel planning. As a dual national you can also enjoy added privacy in your banking and investment activities. Combined with an international trust, you can add privacy, asset protection and diversification to your portfolio.

Understanding there are genuine reasons for a second passport is a first important step in regaining control of your life. When you qualify for a second nation's passport, one that comes with no restrictive strings attached, that document can serve as a passport to a new found freedom. It can be your key to a whole new world of free movement, expanded international investment, enhanced asset protection, greater flexibility, and adventure.

You can obtain a citizenship by investment or outright cash purchases (even though more expensive and less available today than in the past), obtain citizenship by right of birth, or by virtue of how long you are living in a country. These are the three most common means of obtaining citizenship which leads to the right of carrying a passport for that nation.

Citizenship gives you full legal right to live in the country, along with the full legal rights and obligations that come with being a citizen. Sometimes the difference between a citizen and someone with permanent or indefinite legal residency is insignificant. For example, in some countries a permanent or indefinite legal resident still has the full right of property ownership and even the right to vote in elections. In other countries, the rights can be more restrictive, and this varies greatly amongst countries.

One of the biggest advantages of citizenship is the right of traveling on a passport from that country. The value of traveling on a second passport, other than from your homeland country, can be real or perceived. As noted above, Visa free travel to a large number of other countries can be greater, or less, depending on the passport you carry....this is an example of a real benefit.

A real or perceived benefit would be concerns of terrorism threats, or perhaps being more welcomed as a visitor to a foreign country due to being from a more friendly part of the world. Of course it will be a good idea to learn the language or pick up the local accent if you are going to convincingly pull off a charade and not give away your true original domicile or place of origin.

I personally believe the simplest, and perhaps the most important thing to do during international travel is to keep a low profile. Conservative dress, non-threatening mannerisms, low-key speech volume, and interacting with others respectfully, helps avoid disclosing your nationality and place of origin, moving you through the system easily.

Depending on where you are traveling, the loud mouth, demanding, ignorant American, dressed in T-shirt, fanny pack and gym shoes, is generally distained today. As western culture has crossed international borders, the Australian bloke bravado and ill manners is often right behind their Yank cousins.

Our family has found that dressing and acting respectfully, treating others in a respectful manner, speaking softly and in a non-threatening fashion, and with a smile – yes, a smile goes a million miles – is often the best method of travel regardless of what passport you carry. And when appropriate, results can still be accomplished in a passive-aggressive fashion.

Passports and Visas are mostly a new creation of this past century. Historically, a traveler and his property roamed freely from village to village, country to country, subject to the risk of travels during the times. Yes, risk of travel has always existed. And, unless you were held up by robber barons on off-road tracks, you didn't need to take off your shoes or open your bags for inspection…. border check points were pretty rare, at least until this past century.

Passports were originally intended as an introduction of someone of "importance" to a visiting government or other person of prominence. They were never intended to be mandatory identification papers or border passing requirements. On one hand we say we are living on a smaller planet developing into "one village", yet on the other hand, governments continue to unrealistically tighten border restrictions fencing in and out so called "undesirables" looking to freely cross artificial political boundaries.

The free and natural movement of people and property has historically never been so restricted. Today it is done in the name of nationalism, crime, money laundering and terrorism. While these are noble intentions for sure, they are in reality a tiny part of the movement of people and property, and it is all but impossible to restrict the hardcore wrong-doers aimed upon wrong intentions.

In reality, the restrictions on the movement of people and travel by governments are generally motivated by tax generating needs to support a system of entitlements, bureaucracy and global expansion (military and otherwise). Pre-9/11 regulations and restrictions were severe enough. Following America's awakening to terrorism, freedom of travel by ordinary people and movement of assets is grossly over-regulated and restricted……and from where I sit, it only looks to get worse. Much worse.

I will leave it to you to decide if the restrictions you face today to freedom of travel to your person and property are worthwhile, or an unnecessary interference. I believe basic, natural, human rights, have been wrongly interfered with by over-reaching governments trying to dictate how we live and in support of political agendas.

Arguably a dual citizenship opens up the doors for another choice of domicile. However, as noted above, this can often be accomplished with multiple residencies without dual citizenship. And yes, generally you can have multiple citizenships from as many countries you can qualify for without necessarily living in any of them. There are different roads to cross to accomplish second and third citizenships and different reasons for them.

If your primary purpose for obtaining a second passport is for "novelty" purposes or bragging rights, then it is not worth the time, effort and bother. A passport is merely a travel document acknowledging your citizenship in a country. If you have a concern about terrorism, then obtaining a camouflage passport (i.e. a fake one) will most likely suffice, but never think of using it for legitimate identification purposes as that would be illegal. If your objective is for tax avoidance reasons, keep in mind you could actually make your tax situation worse if proper planning doesn't take place with the country the passport represents.

I don't offer the above for the purpose of discouraging you from obtaining a second citizenship. To the contrary, if you are planning to open new doors and options for the future for you or your family, then a second citizenship can be very valuable. But having a second passport alone shouldn't be the primary objective. Instead, the passport should be the icing on the citizenship cake, so to speak.

And too, you can also purchase an "economic" citizenship. For example, in some Caribbean countries (The Commonwealth of Dominica and St Kitts) you can buy citizenships for a set amount of money. I haven't kept up with the current law changes in these two countries, but Dominica used to be a flat $50,000 for a family, and St Kitts required you to purchase a pre-approved condo on the beach for around $250,000 to obtain citizenship. Both have marginal Visas to other counties, and are therefore of limited value, in my humble opinion. But if expatriation is your main objective, then these would suffice.

Ten years ago it was far easier to buy citizenships around the world, and for much, much less..... but that has all changed thanks to the OECD & FATF and our not-so-kinder and gentler governments.

But beware. I recently learned of a scam in the Dominican Republic (not to be confused with The Commonwealth of Dominica) where a promoter promised for $10,000 he would provide you with a residency document and passport. The promoter gives you a "cedula" (certificate of residence) to inspire confidence. Then he invites you to travel to the DR with your cedula to pick up your passport. When you arrive, he asks for your cedula, and after you've given it to him, he informs you that you'll need to pay an additional $10,000 or so for the passport. You're left with nothing – no cedula and no passport. That's because the DR has no economic citizenship law per se.

When you think of a second passport, don't be mislead about marketing gimmicks to *"live the life you have always dreamed."* Instead, think in terms of what citizenship in another country means and what it can really offer you.

Before we explore an example of how to obtain residency to another country, there is a useful tax provision we will look at briefly for U.S. citizens and tax persons. For those earning income offshore, there is a huge tax break that is available. For now it is safely intact, but for how long is anyone's guess.

CHAPTER SIX

911 Relief – of Another Kind

A unique tax benefit for U.S. citizens and tax residents exists today.

Under Treasury Regulations Section 911, if you work overseas, receive earned income from an employer while working overseas, and meet the domicile and residency requirements, a husband and wife can receive some great tax benefits.

Up until recently a U.S. husband and wife could be exempted from approximately $160,000 in joint earned income along with certain housing exclusions, commonly resulting in approximately $180,000 in earned income exclusions. That means that the first $180,000 in foreign earned income becomes tax free, as far as the U.S. government is concerned.

Unfortunately, without any advance notice, in 2006 Congress concealed changes to this tax code provision in other legislation, which reduced the housing allowances, but the earned income exclusion was still mostly intact. Overseas citizen rights groups and international corporations complained loudly, but the voter numbers are very small.

As a result of heavy campaigning by large corporate donors (who says "pork barrels" don't work?) the U.S. Treasury Department and Internal Revenue Service issued Notice 2006-87, which permits individuals who work outside the United States and live in foreign countries with high housing costs to deduct or exclude a greater portion of their housing costs.

Although U.S. citizens and tax residents are generally subject to U.S. tax on their worldwide income, section 911 of the Internal Revenue Code permits individuals who live and work outside the United States (and meeting certain residency requirements) to exclude from U.S. tax, portions of their earned income and housing costs.

As noted above, the Tax Increase Prevention and Reconciliation Act of 2005 (TIPRA) made several changes to Section 911, one of which effectively placed a very strict limit on the amount of housing costs that could be deducted. TIPRA, however, allowed the Treasury Department authority to adjust the new housing cost limitation based on geographic differences in housing costs relative to housing costs in the United States.

In the Notice, using the approach suggested in the legislative history to TIPRA, the Treasury exercised its authority to increase the housing cost limitation, setting forth new higher housing cost amounts for specific locations. The relief provided by the Notice is retroactive to the effective date of TIPRA.

For now, U.S. citizens and tax residents with offshore earned income and housing allowances can result in tax free income as far as Uncle Sam is concerned.

Before moving offshore you will need the legal right to enter and live in a foreign country. The steps vary from jurisdiction to jurisdictions, but the principles are common. And the requirements are often a moving target as immigration objectives are set and reached. Next we look at one very popular venue for obtaining residency, the Land of the Long White Cloud, New Zealand.

CHAPTER SEVEN

Example of Immigration Requirements for New Zealand

New Zealand is a great place to live, earn, retire, or invest. It is a relatively safe environment and is generally located under the political "radar" screen. I should know, my family and I moved from the U.S. and lived in New Zealand for five years, proudly obtaining New Zealand citizenship.

Naturally, like anywhere on the planet, there are trade-offs to consider.

Since New Zealand has been a popular location to travel and explore, and is often a location of great interest for residency leading to citizenship, I have selected this jurisdiction as an example of how to proceed to relocating you, your family, your business, or your money, to New Zealand.

It is true New Zealand is a great place to live and work, or even start a business, but of course everything is relative. Right now New Zealand is looking for people who have the desire, skills and experience to make a difference to the country. In return, New Zealand offers opportunities to succeed and a lifestyle that makes it all worthwhile.

I have outlined below the basic criteria for the most common entry options. But first, you need to ensure you can answer "yes" to the following questions:

1. Are You Healthy?

2. Are you of Good Character?

3. Do you Have a High Standard of English?

If so, you can continue exploring the options. If not, New Zealand is generally not interested in your application. Your partner and/or your dependent children who are included in your residence application must also be of good health and character. They must also meet English language requirements or pre-purchase English language tuition, which they'll need to take up when they arrive in New Zealand.

Investing in New Zealand is a great way to gain entry into the country. New Zealand welcomes people who'd like to invest there. Investors from overseas can build new connections with the rest of the world and increase their understanding with cultures in the Australasian countries.

To be granted residence under the Investor Category, you need to demonstrate that you could successfully settle in and contribute to New Zealand by showing that you intend to make New Zealand your main home, and you can maintain yourself and your family in New Zealand.

First, you can apply for residence under the Investor Category if you are invited to apply. This means you will be invited to apply if you can show in your Expression of Interest that you:

- have NZ$2 million to invest for five years
- have at least five years' business experience
- are healthy
- are of good character
- meet English language requirements, and you
- are 54 years or younger.

The NZ$2 million to invest must be made up of assets and/or funds which are:

- owned by you or jointly by you and your partner and/or dependent children
- legally earned
- unencumbered, and
- transferable through the banking system

You will need to provide acceptable evidence of the value and ownership of funds and assets when you apply for residence.

You need to have at least five years' business experience to be approved for residency under the Investor Category. The length of business experience is based on at least 30 hours per week. You will be given credit for part-time business experience on a proportional basis, so if you have gained eight years' business experience at 15 hours per week, this would equate to four years' business experience based on a 30-hour week.

If you have New Zealand business experience, you must have gained it lawfully while holding a valid New Zealand work permit, or other lawful authority to work.

You might desire to relocate your business here, and would like to send a key employee to set this up. Or maybe you're the key employee of a business that's relocating to New Zealand, and you want to find out if you're able to come here to do that.

Alternatively, you might be interested in establishing a new business in New Zealand. What business opportunities are there in New Zealand?

New Zealand appeals to foreign investors because it is a safe and stable country with a strong commercial outlook. Many parts of the world suffer economic, religious and political upheavals. Fortunately, New Zealand is free of the turmoil experienced in other countries. The code of business practice is generally straightforward and direct.

Importantly, New Zealand has a democratic political system, a free-market philosophy, and the economy is stronger than it's been for years. New Zealand is geographically isolated from the rest of the world, but this has a big advantage – it's the first country across the International Dateline to greet each new business day. So you would always be ahead of your competition and be able to do business with every other country.

Add the creative and independent approach of many New Zealand entrepreneurs and you have an ideal investment opportunity. The business scene is strong and flourishing.

All of this leads to good investment opportunities and it's a solid basis for establishing a new business.

How can you establish a business in New Zealand? Whether you want to start up a new business from scratch or reinvigorate an existing business in New Zealand, you'll find there is a diverse range of opportunities. Perhaps you want to establish a business in New Zealand, but don't want to live in New Zealand permanently. Or maybe you want to establish a business as part of becoming a New Zealand resident.

There are some definite rules and requirements that business investors from other countries have to meet when they're establishing a business in New Zealand.

Should you decide to come to New Zealand to establish a business without living there permanently, or as the first step to gaining residence under the Entrepreneur Category, you will probably need to apply for a Long Term Business Visa. To be eligible for residence in New Zealand under the Entrepreneur Category, you need to have successfully established, and be self-employed or working in, a business that is benefiting New Zealand.

Once applied for, and gained, a Long Term Business Visa or Permit to establish the business, you can then apply for residence. Or you may have held a Work Permit granted under another category that allowed you to establish your own business and you now want to apply for residence.

If so, you:

- must have established, purchased, or made a substantial investment of at least 25 per cent in a business operating in New Zealand,

- must have been self employed or, if you're a part-owner, have worked in that business for two years before you apply for residence as an entrepreneur, and

- no partner or children could have sought social welfare assistance.

Where you first applied for a Long Term Business Visa or Permit, your application will be declined for residence if:

- your business is different from the one included in your Long Term Business Visa or Permit application and

- fail to meet the business plan requirements and

- the business does not have at least the same level of investment as your original proposal and

- you do not have previous experience in that business.

The good news is that you don't need to have a Long Term Business Permit. If you have a successfully established business that's been operating for two years you can apply directly for a Residence Permit under the Entrepreneur Category.

If you're eligible, New Zealand immigration will write to you to tell you that they have approved your application in principle.

You will also need a Long Term Business Permit to allow you to set up and operate your business once you arrive in New Zealand.

Another pathway into New Zealand is under various "Worker" categories. There are four main entry options available to people who wish to come to New Zealand to live and work.

As a Skilled Migrant, you are already suitably qualified and experienced. This option allows you to make an enormous contribution to an innovative and responsive New Zealand workforce, and in turn, help the economy achieve sustainable growth. If you have 'get up and go' and the skills needed, you could be just what New Zealand is looking for.

Can you say "yes" to the first question and to most of the others?

- Are you under 56?
- Do you have a tertiary or trade qualification?
- Do you have at least two years work experience?
- Have you been offered a job in New Zealand?

The Work to Residence entry option could be for you if, for example, you are qualified in a highly specialized or in demand field, or have an exceptional talent in sports or the arts. You can apply for a work permit under the work to residence category, as it allows you to work temporarily in New Zealand as a step towards gaining permanent residence. After two years you can apply for permanent residence.

To qualify, you must either have:

- A genuine offer of full-time, ongoing employment from a New Zealand accredited employer with a base salary of at least NZ$45,000 per annum, or
- Sponsorship from a New Zealand arts, culture or sporting organization because of your reputation and ability to contribute to New Zealand's future, or
- A genuine offer of full-time, ongoing employment in an occupation on the Long Term Skilled Shortage List. You must be aged 55

years or younger, and hold appropriate full or provisional registration if required to practice in that occupation.

Another option is to come to work in New Zealand for a particular event and stay if you have a job offer from a New Zealand employer, or just gain some work experience. Working holidays, work experience or simply sampling life in another country, are all reasons people come to New Zealand to work temporarily.

You can apply for a Temporary Work Permit if you:

- Have an offer of a job from a New Zealand employer and are skilled in an occupation that's in demand

- Want to work in New Zealand temporarily for a particular purpose or event, such as a tournament, a show or for certain professional reasons

- Are a student or trainee wanting to gain work experience in New Zealand

- Are planning to work temporarily while joining your partner in New Zealand

New Zealand has agreements with over 20 countries (including the UK and USA) which allow young people aged between 18 and 30 the opportunity to travel around New Zealand and work temporarily. A working holiday is a great way to get a real taste of life in New Zealand. In most cases, eligible people will be issued with a 12 month Visa and depending on which country you come from, there will be specific requirements you need to meet. Australians have an even easier pathway into New Zealand due to its special relationship with its neighbor across the ditch.

Another pathway into New Zealand is being sponsored by a family member who is already a New Zealand citizen or resident. You must be in one of the groups shown below:

- Partner – you want to come and join your New Zealand partner or you may already be in New Zealand and wish to sponsor your partner

- Dependent Child – you want to come and join your New Zealand parent

- Parent – you want to come and join your New Zealand child or you may already be in New Zealand and wish to sponsor your parent

- Brother, sister or adult child – you want to come and join your New Zealand brother, sister or adult child or you may already be in New Zealand and wish to sponsor your brother, sister or adult child

There are some other specialty categories for immigration into New Zealand, so I will mention them briefly.

There is a special relationship with Samoan neighbors. As part of this special relationship, each year a certain number of Samoan citizens are invited to apply for residence under the Samoan Quota Scheme.

If you are from the Pacific Islands (Fiji, Tuvalu, Tonga or Kiribati), a number of opportunities are offered each year for people to move and live in New Zealand.

The Minister of Immigration has approved a Special Zimbabwe Residence Policy for Zimbabwean nationals who arrived in New Zealand on or before 23 September 2004, and who are not eligible for residence under existing residence policies.

You may like to consider the many different ways you can apply to come to New Zealand for a short time to visit or study or to go there to live or work. The categories and required qualifications change from time to time, so don't be disenchanted if you don't qualify today.

Once you have obtained residency in New Zealand, like many other countries, you can then apply for citizenship. The required time frame for citizenship in New Zealand was recently changed from three to five years.

Surprising to many, is that dual citizenship is perfectly legal in many countries. We will look closer at the historical development of U.S. dual citizenship next, keeping in mind that frequently other western cultures follow the leader, for better or for worse.

CHAPTER EIGHT

The History of Dual Citizenship for U.S. Citizens

Too frequently I am asked if U.S. citizens "really" have a right to hold dual citizenship. Many are puzzled and even surprised that this right exists. As noted above the answer is clearly "yes."

The leading case establishing the right for U.S. citizens to hold dual citizenship is *Afroyim v. Rusk*, 387 U.S. 253 (1967). This 1967 Supreme Court case clearly set the path for U.S. citizens to hold dual nationalities (see summary following historical development below).

For those interested in an historical outline of the development of the major U.S. laws establishing dual citizenship rights, I have included the following section. As a student of history, I enjoy seeing how things develop to a point-in-time, and then seek some insight as to where we might be headed for the future. Admittedly, making sausage and making law can both be a boring and disgusting process, but I guess it is all in your perspective. If you don't enjoy the same historical analysis as I do, then feel free to skip ahead to the next section.

U.S. v. Wong Kim Ark, 169 U.S. 649 (1898)

Wong Kim Ark was born in San Francisco to Chinese parents in 1873. In 1895, upon his return from a visit to China, he was refused entry by U.S. customs officials, who asserted that he was a subject of the Chinese emperor and not a U.S. citizen.

At this time, U.S. law (the "Chinese Exclusion Acts") prohibited Chinese immigration (except for those Chinese people who were already in the U.S.). Chinese people were also barred from becoming naturalized U.S. citizens – and it was argued, on this basis, that Wong was ineligible to be considered a U.S. citizen, in spite of his having been born in the U.S.

The Supreme Court disagreed, ruling on a 6-2 vote that Wong Kim Ark was in fact a U.S. citizen. The court cited the "citizenship clause" of the 14th Amendment, which states that all persons born (or naturalized) in the United States, and subject to the jurisdiction thereof, are citizens. Although the original motivation for this language in the 14th Amendment was to secure citizenship for the freed Negro slaves, the court held that the clause clearly applied to "all persons", regardless of their race or national origin.

The court outright rejected the idea that the Chinese could be singled out for special treatment in this respect. "To hold that the fourteenth amendment of the constitution excludes from citizenship the children born in the United States of citizens or subjects of other countries," the majority wrote, "would be to deny citizenship to thousands of persons of English, Scotch, Irish, German, or other European parentage, who have always been considered and treated as citizens of the United States."

Perkins v. Elg, 307 U.S. 325 (1939)

Marie Elizabeth Elg was born in the U.S. to Swedish parents, who took her back with them to Sweden when she was a baby. Shortly after her 21st birthday, she obtained a U.S. passport and returned to the U.S.

Some years later, the U.S. government attempted to deport her on the grounds that when her parents had taken her to live in Sweden, she had become a Swedish citizen (under Swedish law), and as a result had lost her U.S. citizenship. It was argued that an 1869 citizenship treaty between the U.S. and Sweden, providing for the orderly transfer of citizenship by immigrants, called for loss of U.S. citizenship following Swedish naturalization.

The Supreme Court ruled, unanimously, that the actions of Elg's parents in obtaining Swedish citizenship for their daughter could not prevent her from reclaiming U.S. citizenship and returning to the U.S. as an adult, provided she did so within a reasonable time after reaching adulthood.

The *Elg* case is not, strictly speaking, a dual citizenship case, since the court's assumption was that once Elg had reached adulthood, she had the right to choose U.S. citizenship instead of (not in addition to) Swedish citizenship – i.e., that this right had not been taken away from her by actions her parents had taken when she was a child.

Further, the law as it existed at the time did not, in fact, require Elg (who was born on U.S. soil) to make an "election" of U.S. citizenship (i.e., swear allegiance to the U.S. and return to live there) upon reaching adulthood. The Supreme Court later ruled in *Mandoli v. Acheson* that a U.S.-born dual U.S./Italian citizen could keep his U.S. citizenship despite not having made any such declaration. The issue was not really central to the Elg case anyway, because Elg did get a U.S. passport and moved back to the U.S. before her 22nd birthday.

Kawakita v. U.S., 343 U.S. 717 (1952)

Tomoya Kawakita was a dual U.S./Japanese citizen (born in the U.S. to Japanese parents). He was in Japan when World War II broke out, and because of the war was unable to return to the U.S. During the war, he actively supported the Japanese cause and abused U.S. prisoners of war who had been forced to work under him. After the war, he returned to the U.S. on a U.S. passport, and shortly thereafter he was charged with (and convicted of) treason for his wartime activities.

Kawakita claimed that he had lost his U.S. citizenship by registering in Japan as a Japanese national during the war, and as a result he could not be found guilty of treason against the U.S. Presumably, the reason Kawakita fought so tenaciously *not* to be considered a U.S. citizen was that he saw this as the only way to escape a death sentence for his treason conviction.

However, the Supreme Court ruled that since Kawakita had dual nationality by birth, when he registered himself as Japanese, he was simply reaffirming an already existing fact and was not actually acquiring Japanese citizenship or renouncing his U.S. citizenship.

The court acknowledged that a dual citizen, when in one of his countries of citizenship, is subject to that country's laws and cannot appeal to his other country of citizenship for assistance. However, even when the demands of both the U.S. and the other country are in irreconcilable conflict – such as in wartime – a dual U.S./other citizen must still honor his obligations to the U.S. even when in the other country.

Although Kawakita lost his appeal, his death sentence was eventually commuted by President Eisenhower. He was released from prison, stripped of his U.S. citizenship, and deported to Japan.

Mandoli v. Acheson, 344 U.S. 133 (1952)

Joseph Mandoli was a dual U.S./Italian citizen by birth (born in the U.S. to Italian parents). He left the U.S. as an infant and moved to Italy with his parents. When he sought to return to the U.S. in 1937, his claim to U.S. citizenship was rejected because he had failed to return promptly to the U.S. upon reaching the age of majority, and also because he had served briefly in the Italian army in 1931.

The Supreme Court ruled that the law, as it then stood, did not permit natural-born U.S. citizens to be stripped of U.S. citizenship for failing to return to the U.S. upon reaching adulthood.

The court did not base its ruling in this case on any overriding constitutional arguments. Rather, it examined the legislative history of the portions of U.S. citizenship law, and concluded that Congress had consciously chosen to make these provisions applicable only to naturalized U.S. citizens.

In particular, the court noted that although U.S. law at that time required certain U.S. citizens with childhood dual citizenship (such as those born abroad to American parents) to make a specific "election" of U.S. citizenship (i.e., a declaration of allegiance followed by a return to the U.S.) upon reaching adulthood, no such requirement applied to a person who had U.S. citizenship on account of having been born in the U.S. Lower courts had apparently interpreted the Supreme Court's earlier decisions as imposing such an "election" requirement quite broadly.

The court also decided that Mandoli's foreign military service did not warrant loss of his U.S. citizenship because, under Mussolini's Fascist government, he really didn't have another choice other than to join the Italian army.

Perez v. Brownell, 356 U.S. 44 (1958)

Clemente Perez, a native-born U.S. citizen, moved to Mexico prior to World War II, and remained there for most of the war, in defiance of his legal obligation to register for U.S. military service. While living in Mexico, he entered the U.S. on two occasions, claiming to be a native-born Mexican citizen seeking temporary work as an alien. He was eventually stripped of his U.S. citizenship for evading military service, and also because he had voted in a Mexican election.

The Supreme Court ruled, 5-4, that Congress had the power to revoke the citizenship of Americans who voted in foreign elections, in order to avoid embarrassment in the conduct of foreign relations.

The court rejected the notion that the 14th Amendment's "citizenship clause" restricted Congress's power to revoke citizenship. And it chose not to deal at all with the question of whether citizenship could be withdrawn for remaining outside the U.S. to avoid military duty.

The holdings in the *Perez* case were repudiated by the Supreme Court nine years later, in *Afroyim v. Rusk*.

Trop v. Dulles, 356 U.S. 86 (1958)

Albert Trop, a native-born citizen, was convicted of desertion while a private in the U.S. Army during World War II. He was sentenced to three years of hard labor and dishonorably discharged. Some years later, his application for a passport was rejected on the grounds that he had lost his citizenship due to his desertion.

The Supreme Court, by a 5-4 vote, struck down the relevant provision in the Immigration and Nationality Act. In three separate concurring opinions, various justices proposed that citizenship could not be taken away by Congress at all; or, even if it can sometimes be revoked, it was unacceptable to give such power to military authorities.

Schneider v. Rusk, 377 U.S. 163 (1964)

Angelika Schneider was born in Germany. She came to the U.S. with her parents and became a U.S. citizen upon their naturalization. While a graduate student in Europe, she met a German man whom she later married, and she moved permanently to Germany to live with him.

The State Department claimed Schneider had lost her U.S. citizenship in accordance with a section of the Immigration and Nationality Act, which revoked the citizenship of any naturalized citizen who returned to his or her country of birth and remained there for at least three years. Schneider took the State Department to court ("Rusk" was Dean Rusk, Secretary of State in the Johnson administration) and won her case before the Supreme Court in a 5-3 decision.

The Supreme Court held that since no provision of the law stripped natural-born Americans of their citizenship as a result of extended or permanent residence abroad, it was unconstitutionally discriminatory to apply such a rule only to naturalized citizens. The court rejected arguments that naturalized citizens who resumed permanent residence in their countries of origin presented particular challenges to U.S. foreign policy, and that the government had a right to strip such people of their U.S. citizenship in order to safeguard the country's diplomatic objectives.

Then finally, in 1967 the Supreme Court attempted to settle the issue of dual nationality, which U.S. citizens rely upon today.

Afroyim v. Rusk, 387 U.S. 253 (1967)

Beys Afroyim was a naturalized U.S. citizen, originally from Poland, who moved to Israel in 1950. He tried to renew his U.S. passport in 1960, but the State Department refused on the grounds that he had lost his citizenship by voting in an Israeli election in 1951. Afroyim sued the State Department, and the Supreme Court ruled (5-4) that he was still a U.S. citizen.

The basic point of the Supreme Court's ruling in _Afroyim v. Rusk_ was that the 14th Amendment to the US Constitution – while originally intended mainly to guarantee citizenship to freed Negro slaves and their descendants – had _effectively elevated citizenship to the status of a constitutionally protected right_. Hence, Congress had no right to pass a law which had the effect of depriving an American of his citizenship without his assent.

Thus, the court ruled, a section of the Immigration and Nationality Act mandating automatic loss of citizenship for voting in a foreign election was invalid. Other, similar provisions providing for loss of citizenship for serving in a foreign army, or even swearing allegiance to a foreign country, were similarly invalid unless the action was accompanied by intent to give up U.S. citizenship.

By ruling as it did in the _Afroyim_ case, the Supreme Court explicitly threw out the principles held nine years earlier in _Perez v. Brownell_.

The Supreme Court's _Afroyim_ ruling did not definitively throw out all prohibitions against dual citizenship in the U.S. Although the court clearly stated that loss of citizenship required the individual's assent, some uncertainty remained as to whether an actual swearing of allegiance to a foreign country would, by itself, constitute such assent. (The question of how, or even whether, Afroyim had become a citizen of Israel, or sworn allegiance to Israel, did not come up in his case.)

Also, the court did not address the issue of what standard of proof would be required in citizenship cases – i.e., whether intent to give up citizenship had to be proved clearly and convincingly (as in a criminal trial), or by a preponderance of evidence (as in a lawsuit). This question would not be resolved until *Vance v. Terrazas* (see below).

Rogers v. Bellei, 401 U.S. 815 (1971)

Aldo Mario Bellei was born in Italy in 1939 to an Italian father and an American mother. At birth, he acquired both Italian and U.S. citizenship.

In the 1960's, he was notified that he had lost his U.S. citizenship under a provision of the Immigration and Nationality Act that said a foreign-born U.S. citizen would lose his citizenship unless he moved to the U.S. and lived there for at least five years prior to reaching his 28th birthday.

Bellei took the State Department to court, challenging the validity of the law. However, he lost in the Supreme Court by a 5-4 decision. The majority (including three justices who had dissented in *Afroyim v. Rusk*), upheld the validity of the residency rule and held that the 14th Amendment's citizenship clause, central to the court's ruling in *Afroyim*, did not apply to people acquiring U.S. citizenship by virtue of being born outside the U.S. to an American parent.

Four justices (including three who had been in the majority in *Afroyim*), dissented, claiming that the majority was effectively abandoning the ruling in the earlier case. Bellei is not too significant nowadays, since the provision under which he lost his U.S. citizenship was repealed in 1978 (Public Law 95-432).

Federal Law in the U.S. arises not only by Supreme Court decisions as outlined above, but also by statutory or regulatory law. One such statutory provision that helps define dual citizenship was Section 349 of the INA [8 USC § 1481] which specifies several conditions under which U.S. citizenship may be lost. These include:

- becoming a naturalized citizen of another country, or declaring allegiance to another country, after reaching age 18;

- serving as an officer in a foreign country's military service, or serving in the armed forces of a country which is engaged in hostilities against the U.S.;

- working for a foreign government (e.g., in political office or as a civil servant);

- formally renouncing one's U.S. citizenship before duly authorized U.S. officials; or

- committing treason against, or attempting or conspiring to overthrow the government of the U.S.

The primary effect of recent developments in the U.S. regarding dual citizenship has been to add the requirement that loss of citizenship can only result when the person in question *intended* to give up his citizenship. At one time, the mere performance of the above (or certain other) acts was enough to cause loss of U.S. citizenship; however, the Supreme Court overturned this concept in the *Afroyim* and *Terrazas* cases, and Congress amended the law in 1986 to require that loss of citizenship would result only when a potentially "expatriating" (citizenship-losing) action was performed voluntarily and "with the intention of relinquishing United States nationality."

On 10 October 1978, President Carter signed Public Law 95-432 (92 Stat. 1046; 1978 U.S. Code Congressional and Administrative News 2521). This bill repealed several provisions which had previously allowed revocation of U.S. citizenship.

Some of the provisions abolished by Pub.L. 95-432 had already been rendered unenforceable by the Supreme Court. For example, the bill repealed provisions revoking citizenship for voting in foreign elections (*Afroyim v. Rusk*), moving abroad following naturalization (*Schneider v. Rusk*), and desertion from the armed forces during wartime (*Trop v. Dulles*).

Certain other provisions were also repealed, however, not because of adverse Supreme Court rulings, but because (judging from the legislative history) Congress appears to have decided these provisions were rarely used and/or were not worth keeping. For example, Pub.L. 95-432 repealed provisions revoking citizenship of foreign-born U.S. citizens who failed to move back to the U.S. as adults (a rule *upheld* by the Supreme Court in *Rogers v. Bellei*); children who failed to move back to the U.S. as adults after their parents had lost or given up U.S. citizenship (a weaker version of the rule previously struck down in *Perkins v. Elg*); and dual nationals who lived abroad and had voluntarily claimed benefits of a foreign citizenship as adults. It should be noted that the abolition of these provisions was not made retroactive; people who had lost U.S. citizenship under these provisions did not automatically get it back.

Vance v. Terrazas, 444 U.S. 252 (1980)

Laurence Terrazas was a dual U.S./Mexican citizen by birth (born in the U.S. to a Mexican father). While a university student in Mexico, he signed a document reaffirming his Mexican citizenship. This document contained a section (required by Mexican law) by which Terrazas explicitly renounced his U.S. citizenship.

When the State Department ruled Terrazas was no longer a U.S. citizen on account of this act, he tried to argue in the courts that he hadn't really meant to renounce his U.S. citizenship, despite what was on the Mexican document he had signed. The Supreme Court disagreed (by a 5-4 majority) and held Terrazas to the strict wording of the Mexican document, which it concluded he had understood perfectly well at the time he had signed it.

The *Terrazas* decision established two major points. First, although intent to give up U.S. citizenship could be ascertained either from an individual's specific statements or by inference from his actions and conduct, the "assent" principle of *Afroyim v. Rusk* required that intent to be proved separately from a potentially expatriating (citizenship-losing) action. Congress could not sidestep the issue of intent by declaring a certain action to be inherently incompatible with keeping U.S. citizenship, and then decreeing that voluntary performance of such an action conclusively proved intent to give up citizenship.

Second, although intent to give up citizenship had to be proved, Congress was free to establish the standard of proof. Specifically, it was OK for such intent to be established via a "preponderance of evidence" standard (as in a lawsuit). It was *not* constitutionally necessary for a loss-of-citizenship case to be treated like a criminal trial, requiring intent to be proved by "clear and convincing" evidence.

The *Terrazas* holding regarding intent was eventually incorporated into the text of the Immigration and Nationality Act by Congress in 1986 (Public Law 99-653).

On 14 November 1986, President Reagan signed Public Law 99-653 (100 Stat. 3655; 1986 U.S. Code Congressional and Administrative News 6182). This bill amended the INA to conform to the requirements of various Supreme Court decisions on loss of U.S. citizenship.

The most significant change made by Pub.L. 99-653 was to the preamble of Section 349 of the Immigration and Nationality Act [8 USC § 1481]. The revised wording made it clear that an action, in order to result in loss of citizenship, needed to be performed voluntarily and with the intention of giving up U.S. citizenship.

On 16 April 1990, the State Department adopted a new policy on dual citizenship, under which U.S. citizens who perform one of the potentially expatriating acts listed above are normally presumed not to have done so with intent to give up U.S. citizenship. Thus, the overwhelming majority of loss-of-citizenship cases nowadays will involve people who have explicitly indicated to U.S. consular officials that they want to give up their U.S. citizenship.

Action and Deltamar v. Rich, 951 F.2d 504 (2nd Cir. 1991)

The following 1991 case seems somewhat more in line with the current State Department policy that loss of U.S. citizenship occurs only when a person truly intends to give it up.

Marc Rich, defendant in a multi-million-dollar business lawsuit, contended that the Federal District Court which had heard his case lacked jurisdiction because he (Rich) had given up his U.S. citizenship in 1982 when he became a naturalized citizen of Spain. The Spanish naturalization oath he took included an explicit renunciation of U.S. citizenship.

The Second Circuit Court of Appeals observed, however, that "[D]espite his naturalization as a Spanish citizen, Rich continued to behave in a manner consistent with American citizenship. . . . Rich continued to use his American passport despite renunciation of American citizenship. . . ."

Although Rich asserted that his Spanish naturalization conclusively established his intent to relinquish U.S. citizenship, the court said there "must be proof of a specific intent to relinquish United States citizenship before an act of foreign naturalization or oath of loyalty to another sovereign can result in the expatriation of an American citizen. . . . Despite mouthing words of renunciation before a Spanish official", the court continued, Rich "brought a Swiss action as an American national, traveled on his American passport, and publicized himself in a commercial register as a United States citizen."

Accordingly, the Second Circuit ruled that despite Rich's actions, he had retained his U.S. citizenship because he had never truly intended to relinquish it.

Miller v. Albright, 523 U.S. 420 (1998)

Lorelyn Miller was born in the Philippines to an American father and a Philippine mother (who were not married). She later moved to the U.S. and applied for a U.S. passport, but was turned down on the grounds that she was not a U.S. citizen. Her father signed an affidavit acknowledging his paternity, but this was rejected because he had not signed it prior to Miller's 21st birthday.

Section 309(a) of the Immigration and Nationality Act [8 USC § 1409(a)] says that a non-U.S.-born child born out of wedlock to an American father and a foreign mother can qualify for U.S. citizenship if the father's paternity is established prior to the child's 18th birthday. Prior to 1986, however, this section was operative until the child's 21st birthday, and Miller was able to claim the benefit of the earlier version of the law (though even this didn't help her).

Miller challenged INA § 309(a), claiming that it was unconstitutional to deny her U.S. citizenship because her American parent was her father, rather than her mother. The Supreme Court disagreed and upheld the law on a 6-3 vote.

Any speculation that a slightly different set of facts might have led to a ruling more favorable to illegitimate would-be citizens was laid to rest by the Supreme Court's ruling in *Nguyen v. INS* (see below).

Nguyen v. INS, 533 U.S. 53 (2001)

Tuan Anh Nguyen was the Vietnamese-born illegitimate son of an American father (Joseph Boulais) and a Vietnamese mother. Shortly before his 6th birthday, he was brought to the U.S. and was raised by his father.

After two felony convictions, Nguyen was judged to be deportable, but he challenged this determination by claiming he had U.S. citizenship via his father. The INS rejected Nguyen's claim to citizenship because the requirements 309(a) [8 USC § 1409(a)] had not been satisfied. (Boulais did have a DNA test and obtained a Texas state court ruling identifying him as Nguyen's father, but this did not happen until 1998, well after Nguyen's 18th birthday.)

The *Nguyen* case was accepted for review by the U.S. Supreme Court, and oral arguments were heard by the court in early January 2001. In June 2001, the Supreme Court upheld the lower court ruling, denying Nguyen's claims to citizenship in a 5-4 decision.

U.S. v. Ahumada Aguilar, 189 F.3d 1121 (9th Cir. 1999); *vacated and remanded*, 533 U.S. 913; *on remand*, 295 F.3d 943 (2002)

Ricardo Ahumada Aguilar was the Mexican-born illegitimate son of a Mexican mother and an American father (who left the mother shortly before Ahumada's birth and who had no subsequent contact with mother or son). The mother eventually married a U.S. citizen and immigrated to the U.S. with her son. She made repeated unsuccessful attempts to locate the father of her child, eventually discovering that he had died.

Ahumada was convicted in the U.S. of cocaine possession and was deported. He was subsequently convicted on charges arising from two subsequent illegal entries to the U.S.

Ahumada argued that he was not guilty of illegal entry because he was in fact a U.S. citizen. The trial court rejected this argument because there was no evidence that Ahumada's biological father had ever satisfied the requirements of 309(a) [8 USC § 1409(a)], in that his father had never agreed to provide financial support, and his paternity had never been formally acknowledged.

A three-judge panel of the Ninth Circuit Court of Appeals reversed the trial court's ruling and vacated Ahumada's conviction. The appeals court ruled that the more stringent citizenship requirement for an illegitimate child of an American father – as opposed to an illegitimate child of an American mother – constituted unacceptable discrimination on the basis of gender. In effect, the appeals court ruled that Ahumada was a U.S. citizen after all – which meant that both his deportation and subsequent charges of entering the U.S. illegally were null and void.

The appeals court relied on the sharply divided Supreme Court decision in *Miller v. Albright* – concluding that Ahumada had standing to challenge the gender discrimination of INA § 309(a) because his American father (unlike Miller's) was dead and thus could not mount a challenge himself.

Subsequent to this decision, the Supreme Court upheld INA § 309(a) in *Nguyen v. INS*; and in 2001, the Supreme Court vacated the Ninth Circuit's decision in *Ahumada* and sent the case back for further consideration.

On 1 July 2002, however, the appeals court again vacated Ahumada's conviction for illegal entry to the U.S. The citizenship question had, of course, been settled by the Supreme Court, but the Ninth Circuit found (via an entirely different line of reasoning) that serious flaws in the government's handling of Ahumada's original deportation could reasonably have led him to believe that he could in fact legally attempt to return to the U.S. Whether this latest decision in the *Ahumada* case will survive further appeal (to the full Ninth Circuit, or to the Supreme Court) remains to be seen.

Based upon the big picture, I believe you can fairly conclude that at one time acquiring and keeping U.S. citizenship was a tough and winding road. However, of recent, trying to "shake off" a U.S. citizenship appears to be the more difficult challenge..... as the U.S. government tightens its grip around its tax-income stream to struggle with paying off expensive social entitlements, military expansion, and other budgetary requirements.

Today, pre-migration planning and using international trusts are an essential part of the process before making a move "offshore." Let's look at how this works next.

INTERNATIONAL TRUSTS & PRE-MIGRATION PLANNING

We must not confuse dissent with disloyalty.
When the loyal opposition dies, I think the soul of a nation dies.
Edward R. Murrow

CHAPTER NINE

Pre-Migration Planning

One of the very best ways to help avoid or minimize double tax obligations is through proper pre-migration planning. Theoretically, if you plan ahead properly and take the correct steps, you could actually remove your assets and income from all taxing bodies. In practice, however, that might be a challenging goal to achieve.

Pre-migration planning, simply stated, is considering all steps necessary to accomplish a specific goal of moving self and/or assets *offshore* before taking action. One goal may be to relocate yourself physically to a dream destination. For someone else it might mean availing themselves to global investment opportunities not found at home. To others it is asset protection and wealth preservation. Another often overlooked and less glamorous goal is taking steps to legally minimize income tax obligations. Understanding needs *before* taking action is what pre-migration planning is about.

Trusts have been around in one form or another for at least 2,000 years. The early Roman soldiers who owned property and possessions strode off to war entrusting their assets in the care of someone else in case they failed to return from battle. If they returned, they would take back control and possession of their property. And if they didn't return, the property and possessions were to be distributed as they earlier directed. In the interim, they left specific instructions on how to maintain and preserve the assets. The Romans soldiers of 2 millenniums ago established the first and earliest trust arrangements to be historically recorded.

The use and laws of trusts became more refined and developed by the British.

Hundreds of years ago, Brits were settling trusts for purposes of managing risks and wealth preservation. Even before the Brits, trusts started becoming refined during the Christian Crusades when the knights went off to war in the Middle East ... sound familiar? Later, as the British Empire expanded and conquered the world during the 1800s, the concepts of trust law traveled with them as the new colonies incorporated the British legal system. These newly conquered British lands, and the newly founded United States of America, adopted the trust system as it was then known.

In principal, well-developed trust law concepts allowed someone to place their assets into a trust to keep it segregated from the claims of creditors and others, so long as the assets in the trust were not collateralized or previously subject to the claims of third-parties. "Self-settled" trusts – a trust created by someone intending to benefit from the trust assets – became a common method of protecting one's assets many generations ago, and long before the thirteen original colonies were founded in the U.S.

As these things sometimes go, the law of trusts in the U.S. diverged from the founding principles of well-settled British trust law that had spread around the world. In particular, the U.S. courts took a different point of view in using self-settled trusts for reasons of protecting one's assets and would not allow the wealthy to set aside assets from creditors claims, even though the assets were free from claims when first established. In essence, the U.S. legal system diverged from long standing trust law legal precedent.

Australia, Canada, New Zealand, and Britain today, for example, have all evolved in various ways from the original trust concepts of days gone by…. but the basic trust law principles survive.

The good news is that there are plenty of jurisdictions around the world founded upon long-settled British trust law allowing you to segregate assets from the claims of others by using a self-settled trust. You just need to know how to use and understand the trust principles of these jurisdictions to make them work to your benefit.

A trust is an important tool in accomplishing many different types of objectives. I explored the use of international trusts for asset protection planning at great length in my book *How to Legally Protect Your Assets*. If you are interested in taking a peak at the contents in the book, visit the web site at www.DavidTanzer.com, go to the link at Past Articles on the left, and you will find the Table of Contents and Introduction to the Book. If you are interested in discovering in greater detail how an international trust can help you protect and preserve your assets, this would be a good place to start.

A properly established international trust offers outstanding asset protection planning, worldwide. While this is often the motivating force for many individuals, often times, the pre-migration planning aspect is only appreciated after the fact.

An "international trust" is a term I prefer to use to describe a trust created and registered outside of a home jurisdiction. These trusts are known by many names and are sometimes called "offshore trusts." Remember, everywhere else is, "offshore."

Unfortunately, high-tax jurisdiction governments looking to tax the pants off of you have misaligned and defamed the name "offshore" in the popular media trying to accomplish their objectives of scare mongering to keep a close hand over their subjects. Legitimate, legal, trust planning has been around much longer than these misguided bureaucratic policies and administrative busy-bodies, and I am confident trusts will continue to survive long after they are gone.

When using an international trust for pre-migration planning, an essential requirement is to create and pre-settle the trust in a foreign jurisdiction with solid trust law protective provisions. Not only can you benefit from asset protection and wealth preservation properly integrated with estate planning, you have an opportunity to keep income producing assets outside the reach of a newly adopted homeland. However, it is essential this trust is created *before* making a move to another country.

Benefiting from an international trust for pre-migration planning purposes is simply using well-settled legal trust concepts for a specific purpose. As a practical matter, if the trust assets are "after tax" assets (meaning you have already paid income tax on them) why should you be required to pay income taxes on them again when you access them simply because you move to a new address? Doesn't make logical sense to me, but it commonly happens if planning is not correctly done in advance of relocating to a new jurisdiction.

Taking it one step further, generally speaking, if you maintain pre-settled international trust assets offshore, keep the management and control of the trust outside of your newly adopted homeland, and all income is earned elsewhere, income tax obligations generally do not arise in your newly adopted country. Naturally, there are many tax and legal issues to consider, and planning should only be created and administered by a well-qualified team of tax and legal professionals with good experience with offshore trusts and tax laws.

How you set up and use an international trust for pre-migration planning can vary greatly from country to country and person to person. But the basic concept is that you pre-settle your international trust in a foreign jurisdiction with assets prior to taking up your residency in a different jurisdiction from where the trust is established. Thereafter, keep the assets and income outside of your adopted homeland to avoid taxation.

Some jurisdictions have little or no tax laws related to offshore trusts. Other jurisdictions have a very aggressive set of civil law and trust law developed to bring immigrants into the control of the new tax regime. Even small details can become significant issues when the tax collectors have their eye on your assets. Thus, trusts pre-settled with pre-migration planning goals need to address what is required in the new jurisdiction.

A foreign resident non-U.S. citizen can invest huge amounts of money in the U.S. system – tax free. As covered later, there are numerous classes of assets that enjoy a tax free status because the U.S. government desires that they invest their money into the U.S. for a variety of reasons. Foreigners migrating to the U.S. with a pre-settled offshore trust can continue to enjoy various benefits that a U.S. citizen or U.S. tax resident cannot avail to themselves, so long as a trust is timely structured before they become a U.S. tax resident.

In returning to our example of relocating to New Zealand, a pre-settled trust is an excellent pre-planning tool to keep trust assets and income outside of the taxing system..... if done correctly.

New Zealand defines three types of trusts: 1) Qualifying trust, 2) Foreign Trusts and 3) Non-Qualifying Trusts. The test which defines whether a particular trust constitutes a qualifying trust, foreign trust or non-qualifying trust is applied at the time a distribution is made to a beneficiary, whether it be current year income, a distribution of accumulated income capital gains or just settled trust capital. The primary significance of the different type of trusts is in relation to the taxation of the distributions made by the trust.

A Non-Qualifying Trust, from a New Zealand tax regime's perspective, is a trust that would otherwise qualify as a domestic trust, but has not satisfied the obligations under the Income Tax Act, as an "offshore" trust on which settlement *has been* made by a person who has been a tax resident in New Zealand *after* the date of settlement of the trust.

What all of this means is that a Non-Qualifying Trust is an excellent trust vehicle for those moving to New Zealand. When correctly integrated with asset protection and estate planning, you have the best of all worlds.

Other factors to consider with a Non-Qualifying Trust: it is crucial that distributions of income or capital not be made by the trust to its New Zealand tax residents; additional settlements to the trust must not be made after residing in New Zealand; and to avoid any "interest free" loans from the trust to a New Zealand tax resident. There are other requirements to consider, but this gives you the general idea of how you might pre-settle a trust and keep trust income outside of this tax regime.

Another option is to move to New Zealand on a short term basis and avoid becoming a "tax resident" obligated to pay income taxes. Tax residency can occur once you spend the aggregate of 183 days in any one 365 day period. This is not applied on a calendar year, but on a rolling basis. This offers potential opportunities to make New Zealand a second home without falling into tax obligations.

Once in the new tax regime, you can later easily remove yourself from tax obligations. At a minimum, an individual would need to cease personal residency in New Zealand for a period of 325 days in any 365 day period. Naturally, they would also be giving up their place of abode in New Zealand as a requirement.

Such realistic treatment of taxing only residents actually living in New Zealand should cause U.S. citizens to drool with jealousy over this prospect, since they are bound to draconian tax laws that would require they take extreme measures or denounce their U.S. citizenship. Otherwise, they continue in the U.S. tax regime until death.... and likely beyond.

For comparison purposes, Australia provides a similar opportunity as New Zealand to pre-settle a trust offshore before migrating to its shores.

The rules are different, as you would expect. However, unlike New Zealand where trusts are classified on the basis of settlors, the Australian authorities classify trusts in terms of the residence of the trustee, or alternatively, looks at where control or management of the trust is exercised.

Australia has a set of rules called Trust Transferor Rules, which are aimed at stopping Australian tax residents from accumulating assets in foreign trusts. Australian tax law will apply if at any time during the year the trust is managed or controlled from Australia. However, a pre-settled offshore trust, properly administered and conforming to the strict rules, will also provide an opportunity to keep trust asset income outside of the Australian tax regime.

What's more, when a trust structure is set up correctly, money owned by a non-resident entity owned and controlled offshore by the trust can be invested in New Zealand or Australia at favorable tax rates. The income tax calculated to those non-resident entities is at a substantially reduced rate. For example, instead of paying 39% in taxes in New Zealand or Australia on passive income, a non-resident tax of only 2% or 10%, respectively, could result.

Why invest in cash or property in New Zealand or Australia, for example? The offshore non-resident entities may desire to avail themselves to higher yields in well-established AA- rated international banks with Term Deposits (TDs and called Certificates of Deposits in the U.S.) currently yielding 6.5% to 7.5% for 30 day terms. These TDs are presently far superior than the rest of the world is offering for excellent liquidity as a safe investment. Or, you might just like to have the trust money closer to where you live if relocating to Australasia.

Australia has a similar concept of allowing its tax residents to "opt out" of its tax regime by moving elsewhere, with slightly different requirements to New Zealand.

The bottom line is that the entire world treats its citizens far better for tax purposes than does the U.S. Unlike the U.S., which has the most burdensome tax regime worldwide, taxation is generally based upon residency and where income is earned. Any doubt why the U.S. government takes great effort to slander "offshore" jurisdictions that provide its citizens with a better tax deal? Can you see why the free movement of people and assets is increasingly regulated and controlled by the U.S.? And where does this trend point for the future?

Theoretically, someone who uses an intelligent and aggressive travel approach and timed stays in multiple jurisdictions could be a legal resident or citizen of one or more countries (except not a U.S. tax resident), and not be taxed anywhere in the world. This could be accomplished with pre-planning and foresight, and a thoughtful travel schedule.

However, as noted above, U.S. citizens do not share the same freedoms of their neighbors around the world, and is the only country in the world with draconian, overburdening tax laws with taxation on worldwide income, regardless of domicile, legal residency or where the income is earned. At last count the U.S. and Libya were the *only* two countries in the world with such over-whelming restrictive tax laws. And who says the U.S. doesn't keep good company? No offense to Libya citizens intended.

So, as outlined above, two important questions when considering a move to a new country should be 1) what are the legal residency requirements of the new location of choice and 2) what should you consider regarding tax issues related to the new jurisdiction? Once you have outlined these needs, you can safely begin incorporating these issues into your trust structure, known as pre-migration planning.

Another often asked question is how to manage and invest assets through an international trust. Several examples of investing through an international trust are next explored.

CHAPTER TEN

Investing Through an International Trust

I originally authored and posted the following as an article on my Internet site www.DavidTanzer.com for U.S. citizens. In concept, it is also a valid planning technique for Canadians, Australians, New Zealanders, British, Europeans, and most of the remainder of the civilized world, with "tweaking" for local interests. If you are interested in the full article, you can visit the site and look under Past Articles.

Prospective clients frequently ask how an international trust can be used for managing investments. While every situation is different, there are some basic considerations you should follow.

Remember, using an international trust for investment purposes provides a number of financial planning opportunities, one of which is providing you with greater investment diversification from global markets that would not otherwise be available with domestic investments. And too, an international trust may allow you an opportunity to benefit from solid, legitimate tax planning.

Moreover, if privacy is important to you, an international trust can help keep prying eyes and potential busy bodies from knowing your every financial move. An international trust is also an excellent tool to obtain a high level of asset protection.

Finally, estate planning can, and should be, integrated into an international trust for retirement and inheritance purposes. These are just a few of the *reasons* for using an international trust for your investments.

When I first review a new client's personal financial situation, I like to begin with looking at the big picture. This means that a complete listing of all assets, how they are titled, and the value of those assets, is essential. It's like looking at the fish bowl from the outside, rather than getting lost with the details from the inside.

Knowing what planning tools the client has used in the past, and what are in place today, is important. Understanding the objectives sought for the future, is essential. Perhaps the most important question I ask is... Why?

Having a good understanding of what makes a client tick, and why, is critical in making choices for a good planning structure for their investments.

By way of example, let's say that Mr. Investor is a middle-aged man (ever notice how middle-age is always relative to your current age?). He owns a home with $275,000 in equity. He also owns two real estate investment properties with $25,000 equity in one, and $290,000 in equity in the other. Personal property (jewelry, art, etc.) is valued at $35,000. He has been thrifty and accumulated $150,000 in tax-deferred investments (in the U.S. these are typically referred to as IRAs, pensions, and 401Ks), and another $225,000 in various stocks, bonds, and cash, acquired with after tax dollars.

Most of us would say our investor has done fairly well by having a current net worth of approximately $1,000,000. Since he still has earning-power years ahead of him, we will assume that mortgages and other debts will be paid down, after-tax investments over time will grow, and deferred income values will increase. Changes in the types of investments and values in future years are also certain to occur.

For now though, we will take a snapshot of our investor's financial situation based upon today's values. Several examples follow of how he might use an international trust.

Mr. Investor presently owns all of his investments in his name and seeks greater diversification and higher yields. Presently, if Mr. Investor is a U.S. citizen, trading and investment opportunities are limited to only one-third of the world's equity and bond investments. This is due to the stringent and over-burdening U.S. Federal regulations imposed on foreign institutions that simply refuse to deal with U.S. citizen-investors as a result.

If our investor instead used an international trust, he could open the doors to invest in quality equities and bonds in the rest of the world. New banking or trading accounts could be opened through the trust allowing participation in investment grade opportunities that were closed off to our investor before. Our investor and the trust will still be subject to U.S. taxes and compliances issues, but diversification and greater investment opportunities could be achieved if he invested through an international trust.

Our investor also seeks greater protection from losing his real estate investments, his home, stocks, bonds, cash, and other personal property in a litigation-gone-mad-society. Since all of the assets are presently in his name personally – most of which took his lifetime to accumulate – one lawsuit could wipe out everything overnight.

A common misconception is that sufficient insurance will solve any lawsuit concern. But what happens if the claim is excluded from coverage? Or, what happens if the claim is in excess of liability limits? This is not uncommon as juries regularly hand out multi-million dollar awards. Or, even if the claim is covered, what happens if the insurance company goes bankrupt and you are left holding the bag?

Unfortunately, I have witnessed all of these examples occur to unsuspecting good people, time and time again.

It is always a significant risk to hold title to your investments in your own name. The better approach is to control and use your assets from a separate entity, which holds title to the investments. Separating title from control is an essential part in planning to protect your investments. You control; the international trust holds title.

There are pros and cons of the benefits of using domestic planning structures vs. using international planning tools for owning investments. The comparison is not discussed here. But it is sufficient to state that while domestic structures have a benefit – something is always better than nothing – using an international trust for owning and controlling investments is generally far superior for a long list of reasons.

The first example of how Mr. Investor could use an international trust would be to re-title investments and certain other assets into a self-settled, international grantor trust. This means placing title to the home, real estate investments, personal property, and stocks, bonds and cash into the trust. A properly structured international trust could offer significant advantages over holding title to the property in his name. He would still be able to use and maintain control over these investments, consistent with the terms and provisions set forth in the trust documents.

Another common misconception is that using an international trust means transferring investments to an offshore, far away place. While this is always an option for Mr. Investor to consider if he is looking to broaden his investment horizons worldwide, it is not necessary. He can easily maintain his investments exactly where they are located today, with title held in the name of the international trust. As the comfort level increases with investing in other countries, investments can then be moved around globally at ease.

A properly structured international trust could permit Mr. Investor to use and occupy the home, make investment choices concerning the stocks, bonds and cash, and deal with the investment real estate in a similar manner as he had before. He could also readily receive cash distributions from the investments to live off of, if he desired. The big difference is that he is dealing with these assets in the name of the trust, and not in his name. Structure and planning is everything in setting up the international trust to achieve these goals.

A huge benefit in the above example of placing investments into the international trust, is that if Mr. Investor is personally sued, he may have significant opportunities to keep his investments out of the reach of certain classes of creditors. Issues of fraudulent conveyances, collateralized assets, and other legal topics come into play, but are beyond the scope of discussion for now. Still, an international trust is a relatively uncomplicated and a commonly used planning structure for investment purposes… one of which may be to protect them from frivolous creditors.

One drawback to assets held directly by the trust is that if a legitimate lawsuit was filed against the trust arising from one of the real estate investments, all of the other investments and assets in the trust could be subject to the claim. In other words, the investments may be protected from litigation filed against him personally, but there are always risks when a lawsuit is filed directly against the trust with different investment classes of varying degrees of risk.

Even with the above being said, proper planning of an international trust can often significantly mitigate the risk of litigation against the trust directly. If the trust is set up properly, in a timely manner, and if formed in a jurisdiction offering the best asset protection for his investments, Mr. Investor could generally increase his chances of success in the outcome following litigation.

Therefore, the more common use of an international trust to hold all investments is best only when they are all low risk assets, such as stocks, bonds and cash. This class of assets is considered less likely to be the subject of direct litigation as compared to real estate investments or other active business pursuits.

Since Mr. Investor has different types of investments with varying degrees of risk, a far better example would be for him to use an international trust to hold title to various entities. Each entity would hold title to his different types and classes of assets.

It is important to note that proper planning always requires using the proper entity type for a particular investment, often motivated by tax reasons. In the U.S. these are typically referred to as S-Corps, C-Corps, LLCs, and FLPs, and they are only a few of the choices on offer to hold title to assets. All countries offer similar types of entities.

Our investor could still maintain control over the assets, and the title could be removed yet another step away from a frivolous lawsuit. This type of planning offers far greater flexibility than assets being held directly by the trust. The opportunities for diversifying investments, and broader asset protection planning for those investments, can also be accomplished.

A better example would be for our investor to place title to his home in a single member limited liability company, domestic or offshore, which may provide for full tax advantages found in home ownership ... he would be the manager of the LLC, maintaining control and the right of occupancy. This could effectively provide an opportunity for safeguarding the home, $275,000 in equity from the failings of other investments, and most likely maintain the husband and wife capital gains exemption.

Then, the stocks, bonds and cash totaling $225,000 could be held in a family limited partnership, with our investor being the general partner, again with maintaining control over investment decisions. Keeping assets like stocks, bonds and cash separate from riskier assets, like real estate, is generally considered safe and conservative planning. The other personal investment property totaling $35,000 (the jewelry and art) could also be placed within this same entity, so long as none of these assets had high risk factors.

Our investor, in the name of the family limited partnership, could easily make trades within the portfolio. All income could pass through this entity, then through the trust, on to the investor.

However, keep in mind that certain types of investments could have a negative tax consequence if placed into this vehicle, so care must be taken with the type of investments transferred into it.

An important question for our investor to consider would be how to treat the two real estate investment properties. For example, should they both be held in one company? Or, should they be separated into two different companies?

An argument for each real estate investment to be placed into its own entity, is that litigation against the investment with only $25,000 in equity will not expose the other real estate investment with $290,000 in equity. A disadvantage is the cost and additional reporting requirements, which are generally minimal.

Alternatively, our investor could elect to keep both real estate investments into one company today if the lesser equity investment is low risk, and then segregate them in the future if risk intensifies, or as equity value increases. Otherwise, two separate companies (such as an LLC) today would be a risk-adverse choice. Our investor could still continue to manage and make rental decisions as he had before. The main difference is that he would be making these decisions on behalf of the company.

Great care must be taken with transferring investments that are considered tax-deferred. Transferring the $150,000 tax-deferred investments into another entity could, and probably will, trigger negative tax consequences. However, there are some exemptions to this rule, particularly if our investor was in the process of taking distributions at retirement age.

Sounds like you are complicating life when using an international trust for investment purposes?

Not really. I have found repeatedly that once an investor's structure is properly set up, tax advantages are more easily identified and achieved, instead of being overlooked. And too, once an investor gains more confidence in investing beyond the shores of their homeland, diversification and better yields are more easily realized.

An added benefit to using an international trust for investment is that the trust agreement is a private document. It is not filed in a public domain (like company documents or probating Wills), achieving greater levels of privacy. As noted above, integrating retirement planning and estate planning into an international trust is generally part of the planning process for our clients.

Naturally, the terms of the international trust must be carefully drafted, and the entity formalities must always be satisfied. A plan that is "one-size fits all" should be avoided, since it rarely fits anyone.

And importantly, when your international trust structure is created, it needs to be flexible enough to allow it to adjust to your investments and objectives as they change over time.

While there are common themes that run between many investors we consult with regularly, everyone is a little different. Customizing your plan to meet your investment needs is essential to reaching and maintaining investment objectives.

To summarize:

Identify the best international trust structure for you to hold title and maintain control over your assets. Make certain that a qualified professional that can customize a plan to your investment needs creates the structure. Careful planning for flexibility should always be considered to allow your structure to adjust to the changes in your investments, the changes in value, and the changes that occur in life.

One word of caution is in order before you start transfers of everything you own into an international trust. While U.S. asset transfer to a trust can become a technical challenge, it is one you should be aware of to avoid dreadful consequences.

CHAPTER ELEVEN

U.S. Asset Transfers to Trust

We now turn to a technical question: If a U.S. citizen or tax resident transfers equities from his own name to an offshore trust or off-shore annuity, is he liable for capital gains tax or any other taxes?

The answer is "it depends." First, it depends on the nature of the transfer to the trust ... is it a "complete" or "incomplete" transfer? And it depends on whether the trust is a "grantor" or "non-grantor" trust; and whether the trust is considered "domestic" or "foreign" for U.S. tax purposes. And depending on the nature of the transfer and the trust, the final answer will be influenced on whether the equities (presumably securities) have appreciated since they were acquired. This answer involves one of the most complex and ambiguous issues in the international section of the U.S. tax law.

In the case of a transfer of appreciated assets to a foreign insurance company in exchange for a foreign commercial annuity, the gain would be taxable in the same way as if the assets had been sold and then the proceeds were transferred to the foreign insurance company. (The same rule applies to transfers of appreciated assets to a U.S. insurance company in exchange for an annuity or life insurance policy.) There are apparently some promoters who are falsely telling U.S. investors that they can exchange appreciated assets tax free (deferred) for a foreign annuity from a foreign insurance company.

Appreciated assets can be exchanged for a private annuity on a tax deferred basis – but there are a lot of technicalities that must be satisfied. A private annuity is defined as an unsecured contract with a person or company that is not in the business of issuing annuities or life insurance contracts. If the person to whom appreciated assets are given in exchange for an annuity defaults on his obligation, the annuitant has no recourse at all. That's why legitimate private annuities are between a U.S. person and an heir – usually a child or grandchild. There are some technical arguments for and against the concept of using an irrevocable trust to make the annuity payments.

Some promoters are encouraging U.S. taxpayers to transfer highly appreciated assets to a foreign trust or a foreign life insurance policy in exchange for an annuity. A more complex arrangement involves the transfer of appreciated assets to a foreign corporation owned by a foreign insurance company in exchange for a private annuity. In these arrangements, the annuitant is also the insured and policyholder of a variable life insurance policy issued by the insurance company. The IRS disagrees with the views of these promoters and has indicated that they will challenge such arrangements.

As for transferring appreciated assets to a foreign trust, typically the transfer is subject to capital gains tax if the foreign trust is a *non-grantor trust*. The IRS argues that this means the foreign trust must not ever have any U.S. beneficiaries. Some U.S. tax professionals argue that it means the foreign trust must not have any U.S. beneficiaries for more than a year after the death of the trust grantor and his/her spouse.

Regarding other taxes, there is an excise tax of 1% on the amount of premium paid to a foreign insurance company. When assets are transferred to a foreign grantor trust, the U.S. grantor is subject to income tax on any income earned by the foreign trust.

To avoid negative tax consequences outlined above, our firm recommends a gift tax return (Form 709) be filed by April 15 following the close of each year in which a transfer to a trust or to any of its underlying entities is made. The transfers are then reported as *incomplete transfers,* as defined under U.S. tax law.

For a U.S. domestic *grantor trust* (the type our firm generally recommends), Form 709 is typically informational in nature (with no trust tax due), since under the usual structure established by our firm, any such transfers are incomplete for federal gift tax purposes under Treasury Regulations Section 25.2511-2, and as such there are no gift tax implications.

The requirement for a return to be filed in this situation is set forth in Internal Revenue Code Section 6019, and in Treasury Regulations Sections 25.6019-1(a) 25.6019-3(a), and 25.2511-2(j).

Please note the above comments are an extremely brief summary and involve multiple sections of the tax code and regulations and some court cases. Segments of the above and the following tax matters of foreign trust tax rules from a U.S. perspective are reprinted with permission from Offshore Press.

CHAPTER TWELVE

Foreign Trust Tax Rules From a U.S. Perspective

It used to be legal for U.S. citizens and residents to defer taxes with a foreign trust, if it was an irrevocable trust and if the trust settlor/grantor retained no powers over the disposition of the trust assets. In 1976, the rules were changed and the reasons may become a bit technical to the casual reader, as noted below.

Keep in mind there is an important distinction to make when referring to offshore or international trusts. The offshore or international trusts which qualify as *"domestic trusts"* under the U.S. tax code are very different from a *"foreign trust"* as defined under the U.S. tax code. The reporting requirements and compliance issues are significantly different. And note these differences when reading the following.

After the 1976 changes, because of U.S. Internal Revenue Code Section 679, U.S. persons who form (settle) a foreign trust that has a U.S. beneficiary is treated as the owner of the assets in the trust for income tax purposes. These trusts are described as 'tax neutral' and are used for asset protection from future litigation rather than for tax avoidance. Many of the promoters of phony foreign trusts selling "tax benefit" arrangements are showing their prospective customers outdated laws, regulations or court cases, or showing them nothing to support their claims.

For non-U.S. persons in many countries, it is still legal to avoid domestic income taxes and estate taxes (or forced heirship) with the use of a foreign trust. If that foreign trust is located in a low tax jurisdiction (tax haven), the income earned by the trust assets are treated as the income of the trust rather than of the trust settlor and/or beneficiaries.

There is still one tax advantage to a U.S. person in creating a foreign trust through their will. After the death of a U.S. grantor, a foreign trust ceases to be subject to U.S. income taxes until the funds are distributed to a U.S. person. And, if the trust is established in a country without a statute of limitations, it can be used as a 'perpetual' (dynasty) trust that accumulates and distributes assets to multiple generations. Such a trust can be funded by testamentary disposition or if it is created while the grantor is living, it will cease to be a grantor trust following the grantor's death.

Until some very recent regulations issued by the IRS, most tax professionals believed that it was possible to create a foreign trust so that it would have no U.S. beneficiaries during the lifetime of the grantor and hence it would not be subject to the income tax treatment of IRC Section 679. By creating an irrevocable foreign trust with no U.S. beneficiary during the lifetime of the grantor (or the grantor's spouse), any income accumulated in the trust during the lifetime of the grantor or spouse would not be subject to tax by the U.S. grantor. Nor would the trust assets be included in the estate of the trust grantor or spouse. However, regulations issued by the IRS in September, 2000 indicate that this kind of trust can't ever have any U.S. beneficiary – even after the death of the U.S. grantor and spouse.

Prior to the *U.S. Small Business Job Protection Act of 1996*, it was possible for foreign persons who were migrating to the U.S. to establish a trust in a country outside the U.S. and to avoid the U.S. grantor trust rules. Now, for trusts settled after February 6, 1995, the grantor of a foreign trust will be deemed to have formed the trust on the date he or she becomes a U.S. resident – *unless* the trust was formed at least five years before the residency starting date.

Prior to the 1996 law, a trust was deemed to be a domestic trust or a foreign trust based on the preponderance of facts relating to the administration of the trust, the jurisdiction to which the trust would seek judicial recourse, the residence of the trustee and other related facts. Now, a straight-forward, two-part test is used to determine if a trust is a U.S. domestic trust or a foreign trust. A trust is deemed to be a domestic trust if

1. a U.S. court can exercise primary jurisdiction over the administration of the trust, and if

2. one or more U.S. persons have the authority to control all substantial decisions of the trust.

If a trust does not meet both of these tests, it is deemed to be a foreign trust for U.S. tax purposes. Form 3520 must be filed with the income tax return of the grantor of a foreign trust for each year and

Form 3520-A must be filed with the grantor's tax return each year thereafter. Any U.S. beneficiary of a foreign trust must file a Form 3520 with his or her tax return in any year in which the beneficiary receives a distribution of any kind. Any distribution from a foreign trust to a U.S. beneficiary may be treated as taxable income unless the required reports are filed and substantiate that the distributions are not income to the beneficiary. The penalties for failing to file the reports or for filing late are severe.

Beneficiaries and grantors of a foreign trust are deemed to be the shareholders of any corporations in which the trust is a shareholder or to be the partners of any partnership in which the trust is a partner. If the foreign trust is a 10% or greater shareholder of a controlled foreign corporation, the U.S. grantor is deemed to be the beneficial owner of the foreign corporation and must file the Form 5471 for shareholders of a controlled foreign corporation. If the foreign trust is an investor in a foreign investment company, unit trust or mutual fund, the grantor of the trust is deemed to be a shareholder of a passive foreign investment company and must file Form 8621 with his or her tax return.

To the contrary, an international or offshore trust that qualifies as a domestic trust for tax purposes has significantly reduced reporting requirements, and are much more user friendly, in my humble opinion. For these reasons we generally create international or offshore trusts that qualify as domestic trusts under the U.S. tax code.

Both types of trusts have their place, but we find most of our clients look to keep things less complex and under the I.R.S. radar screen.

With so many benefits to using an international trust, it is surprising there are still some that speak out against them. I think it is now important we dispel some of the myths circulating against using international trusts.

CHAPTER THIRTEEN

Doomsayer Comments Against International Trusts

There are still those that don't believe in using international or off-shore trusts, and believe asset protection planning can be just as effective when formed and maintained within the U.S. I strongly disagree, but include the following section for those interested in the debate.

What follows below is an exchange of correspondence between myself and another attorney in response to his doomsayer's comments against international and offshore trusts he expressed in a recent publication. The lawyer, I call Dr. Doom, argues that U.S. stateside asset protection and boiler plate trusts are most likely just as good as the offshore variety, with the benefit of staying "closer to home" in a familiar environment. The lawyer that wrote the original article was not, in my opinion, particularly well-versed about international trusts in general, or asset protection planning in specific, even though he was selling his services to the public in this area.

The reason I share the following exchange of comments with you is because, unfortunately his comments too frequently reflect the same negative myths too often found in the uninformed popular media selling newspapers and magazines. At least you can get an inside view of the issues as we expressed our opinions. I add my additional comments for your understanding in parenthesis.

First, Dr. Doom states that entering into a foreign trust increases the likelihood of an audit (a very popular myth).

My response:

First, there are two types of foreign trusts: a U.S. Domestic Grantor Trust (for U.S. tax purposes is tax neutral and a compliance-light type of trust, which is the type I recommend), and does not generally increase the likelihood of an audit as compared with a true Foreign Trust, which may increase the likelihood of an audit (for U.S. tax purposes it is a compliance-heavy type of trust, which I do not generally recommend). Dr. Doom, and journalists in the popular media, often make the same mistake by mixing the two up, lumping them together as one, and failing to make an important tax distinction between the two. Most likely he, like most uninformed journalists, is unfamiliar with the distinction between the two since he appears to promote garden variety stateside planning.

Dr. Doom states the *Andersen* and *Lawrence* cases demonstrate that offshore, international trusts used for asset protection planning are ineffective, unless you are willing to go to jail to protect the assets.

My response:

Both of these cases are now over 10 years old and have been beat up and talked about and long been left buried and dead ages ago. Considerable law has evolved in this arena during the past decade. These were two very extreme, high profile cases with which I am familiar (but not as our clients), and it is true both parties were jailed while trying to protect trust assets....but understanding the underlying facts clarifies the problems.

In *Andersen*, the attorney who created the offshore trust, did many things wrong. It has been argued he most likely committed professional malpractice in both structuring the trust and administering it when a problem arose. For example, the *Andersens* acted as trustees and protectors of their own trusts (you never want to do this), even after litigation commenced, availing themselves, the trust and the assets to the jurisdiction of the U.S. courts (a huge mistake).

Thereafter, the *Andersens* refused to comply with a court order directed against them to repatriate assets, then resigned as trustees and protectors, and were jailed for contempt of court for refusing to comply with a court order and creating their own "impossibility" to return the assets following their resignation. The court made it clear the *Andersens* clearly created their own problem with acting in the capacities they did and then resigning instead of complying with the court order .... this is why they were jailed for contempt of court.

Further, Dr. Doom forgets to tell you the FTC (Federal Trade Commission) spent huge amounts of government money in the U.S. Courts and in the Cook Island Courts and *failed* to receive any money awarded by judgment from either of the judges. Moreover, the *Andersen's* attorney's fees were assessed in their favor and *against* the FTC.

In my opinion, this was not a case to cheer the *Andersens* to victory in holding up an international trust, since by all accounts they defrauded many innocent people through a Ponzi scheme. To be sure, the trust and the *Andersens* prevailed in the Cook Islands, but ultimately they settled with the FTC and the Ponzi scheme victims.

As for *Lawrence*, the testimony and the judge's statements in the court proceedings makes it very clear that *Lawrence* repeatedly lied under oath in the courtroom (hiding assets and lying about them is not a hallmark of good asset protection planning), perjuring himself and committing civil and criminal contempt. *Lawrence* was jailed for contempt of court, and he deserved it from what I read in the transcripts.

An Omnibus Order signed by the United States District Court for the Southern District of Florida on December 12, 2006, states that:

Lawrence is a Debtor who was incarcerated for civil contempt based on his failure to comply with a bankruptcy court order to turn over the res of an inter vivos trust to a Chapter 7 trustee in 2000. [During his incarceration] Lawrence has steadfastly refused to comply with this Court's contempt order. Upon examination of the entire record... I now conclude that there is no realistic possibility that he will comply. As such, I am obligated to release Lawrence because the subject incarceration no longer serves the civil purpose of coercion.

This outcome reinforces the legal principle that one of the purposes of contempt of court is to coerce performance when performance is possible. In *Lawrence* the court determined that there was no longer any coercive effect that resulted from Mr. Lawrence's incarceration and Mr. Lawrence was therefore released. While Mr. Lawrence is *not* a client of our firm (and no client of ours has been incarcerated for contempt), our understanding is that the $20 million dollars Mr. Lawrence protected at *the last minute* remains protected and in a Cook Islands trust.

The bottom line is these two cases are terrible examples to argue that asset protection is a problem using an international or offshore trust for U.S. citizens..... like saying if you eat chicken you will get bird flu. Bad facts and bad law are a poor combination to argue against the success of literally thousands and thousands, if not hundreds of thousands, of well planned and maintained trusts, established over past decades.

When creating asset protection planning structures, and international trusts in general, it is essential it is above board, legal, and you are able to testify under oath with confidence that your intentions were strictly honorable.

Next, Dr. Doom refers to certain classes of assets afforded special protection as exempt assets under state and federal bankruptcy laws as a good way to protect assets.

My response:

He is correct, certain classes of assets are afforded protection when a debtor is forced to file for protection under bankruptcy laws.......but having to file bankruptcy to obtain asset protection is not, in my opinion, a hallmark of quality asset protection, which can be better achieved without those extreme measures.

Dr. Doom next argues a technical point about the pros and cons of provisions within trusts giving rise to a distinction between Discretionary Trusts and Spendthrift Trusts, and the development of trust law in this regard.

My response:

While these two types of trust provisions are distinguishable and have their benefits in trust planning, neither offer real protection because of the U.S. prohibition to *self-settled* irrevocable trusts. In general, American jurisprudence does not favor a *self-settled* Discretionary Trust or a *self-settled* Spendthrift Trust. Interesting is how the American jurisprudence system has departed from the British system in this respect (see my comments in the earlier chapter about the historical development of self-settled trusts).

However, by going offshore, outside of the U.S., you <u>can</u> *self-settle* an irrevocable trust for asset protection. Trust law worldwide originates from the traditional British trust law routes – its origins dating back to the Roman armies leaving their assets in trust while going off to battle. Using an international trust allows you to accomplish what cannot be achieved with a typical trust in the U.S.

Dr. Doom says the U.S. states – for example, Alaska and Delaware – offering self-settled Dynasty Trusts for asset protection are just as good, or better, than using an international trust....besides things are safer at home where U.S. citizens are most familiar.

My response:

Alaska and Delaware self-settled Dynasty Trusts demonstrate the U.S. is slowly moving back towards its British trust law roots allowing self-settled trusts for asset protection planning, allowing Americans to do what the rest of the world has done for generations. Domestically, there are now approximately seven states in the U.S. embracing the concept. While we never support the concept of international planning "stateside," it still confirms a shift in the trend with less negative "stigma" attached.

U.S. self-settled trusts are still problematic for quality asset protection, due to many reasons. This includes Conflict of Law Issues between states (when multiple state parties are involved, which state law applies?); Full Faith and Credit Laws (Federal laws requiring judgments in one state be recognized and enforced in another state); results orientated activist judges (increasingly a problem when judges are more concerned in results and not following the law); Fraudulent Conveyances Statutes (easy to unwind a domestic trust transfer unlike in offshore jurisdictions); and the 10 year "look back" provisions under the new Bankruptcy laws (which offshore jurisdictions do not recognize).

If anything, Dr. Doom presents a very good case that asset protection is *not* very good when limited to stateside planning.

Dr. Doom says that *common law* Charging Order protection, first founded in Colorado, is as good as *statutory* Charging Order protection. (For your information, Charging Order Protection prohibits a judgment creditor from forcing the disposition of assets within an entity when owned by a judgment debtor. Colorado was once a popular state for this type of protection until statutory protection was enacted elsewhere.)

My response:

Dr. Doom refers to Family Limited Partnerships having Charging Order protection by virtue of dicta found in an old Colorado court case and "haphazardly" confirmed in the Uniform Limited Partnership Act. This issue was tested in the state courts in the 1990s with not very favorable results. The outcome in one court case was a problem for the client and his attorneys. I have little confidence in Colorado's Charging Order protection and there is far better protection found in legislative statutory provisions in other venues, domestically and offshore. Arizona and Nevis are two excellent examples.

Finally, Dr. Doom says the garden-variety "one size fits all" asset protection trust is probably just as good as the higher priced offshore models, as they will most likely scare off the creditors just as well.

My response:

Asset protection ultimately stands or falls in a courtroom.... this is where it is tested. Today, too frequently, boiler plate asset protection trusts are offered by estate planners with no courtroom experience that have notched up their menu of legal services for their client base. Again, in my humble opinion, when someone with little or no experience in litigation tries to provide asset protection they are in an arena outside of their expertise and usually miss the mark where it is needed most. You have to start with litigation in mind, because that is where you can ultimately end up if, and when, you are sued.

As noted from my above brief responses, too frequently the *misinformed* attempt to lead the *uninformed*. A general medical practitioner is no more qualified to do brain surgery than a local general or estate planning attorney is qualified to structure an international trust. With all respect to the general practitioners, they too are specialists in their own right, but would very seldom be qualified to do international planning.

And where to register a properly drafted international trust?

Those in the know understand that the Cook Islands needs no introduction with respect to its trust laws.... it is considered by many to be second to none. It is true there are other good jurisdictions, however I believe the Cooks stand above the rest.

A Cook Islands International Trust has a number of distinct advantageous features:

- The International Trusts Act of 1984 abolished the perpetuity period rule in the Cook Islands and so enabled the "dynasty" trust to be established and administered in perpetuity.

- The Act has been amended from time to time to keep up with developing international legal issues, and is generally considered the "leader in the industry."

- A trust is not void or voidable in the event of the Settlor's bankruptcy.

- The Act allows the Settlor to retain or acquire a power of revocation of the Trust; a power of disposition over Trust property; a power to amend the Trust Deed; and to retain an interest in the Trust property.

- The only information that must be filed with the Registrar of International Trusts is the name of the International Trust, the names of the trustees and the date of the trust deed. The details of the beneficiaries and settlor of the trust are not registered and the public registries in the Cook Islands are not open to the general public.

- Cook Islands' law will not recognize foreign judgments. Any claimant must commence new proceedings in the Cook Islands, subject to Cook Islands law. Any such proceedings must be brought within 12 months of the settlement or disposition to a trust.

- The Cook Islands do not recognize foreign inheritance laws. If a foreign party from a civil law jurisdiction raised a legal challenge in the local courts against a disposition made by a settlor and cited foreign inheritance laws as the basis of a claim alleging that the disposition was invalid as it offended against the forced heirship rules that applied in his country, the action would fail.

- Only the judgments of New Zealand courts can be enforced in the Cook Islands. A foreign creditor wishing to set aside a disposition would have to commence an action in the courts of the Cook Islands and so put himself within the ambit of laws and procedures which are generally favorable to the settlors, trustees and beneficiaries of an International Trust.

- Exemplary and punitive damages generally are not available in the Cook Islands and would therefore be denied in New Zealand to a litigant even though previously obtained by judgment in a local court.

- The rule against accumulations has been abolished in the Cook Islands. In the Cook Islands the trustee of an International Trust can accumulate the income indefinitely.

- There is no tax liability in the Cook Islands and no requirement to file any returns, reports, or tax records.

- The trust deed can provide for a change in the governing law on the happening of a specified event (otherwise known as a "flee clause").

- The common law rule against purpose trusts has been abolished in the Cook Islands which has provided a mechanism under which a purpose trust can be enforced by the court.

- The definition of what does and what does not constitute a charitable trust has been extended in the Cook Islands.

- Under Cook Islands law a disposition can only be set aside if: a) the disposition occurred within 2 years of the date of the act or omission which gave rise to the creditors cause of action and the creditor can prove fraud on the part of the settlor; or b) if the action to set aside the disposition is commenced within 3 years of the date of the act or omission which gave rise to the creditors cause of action. If an action has already commenced in a foreign court the time limit is frozen pending its conclusion.

- Under the International Trusts Act 1984 the rule requiring unanimity among trustees now only applies to an International Trust if the trust deed does not specify otherwise. The trust deed can now set out procedures for making the majority decisions by the trustees.

- In the Cook Islands a trust deed can provide provisions for a trustee to delegate all powers, except dispositive powers. Therefore, a Cook Islands trustee could place all trust fund investment decisions in the hands of an investment company.

- A trust deed may impose a different standard of care on a trustee making investments. Unless otherwise specified, the standard of care expected of a trustee is that of a prudent person managing the affairs of another. Under the common law, if the trustee is a professional, the standard of care is expected to be higher.

- The law allows for new or redrafted trusts to prescribe a perpetuity period of no longer than 100 years so as to take advantage of the abolition of the perpetuities rule.

- So long as the settlor appoints a licensed and resident Cook Islands trustee as a custodian trustee, he is free to appoint managing trustees within his own jurisdiction, generally referred to as a domestic trustee.

- The trust deed can appoint a "nominated person" who has the power to obtain the consent of and represent all the beneficiaries including non sui juris and future beneficiaries, beneficiaries who cannot be found and beneficiaries who have yet to be ascertained.

- There are provisions allowing trusts to be redomiciled in and out of the Cook Islands. A trust re-domiciled in the Cook Islands is by the Islands' law deemed to be an International Trust formed under the International Trusts Act 1984 from the date of its inception and not just from the date of its re-domiciliation.

- Under Cook Islands law, the trust deed can deem that different aspects of the trust can be governed by the laws of different jurisdictions.

Undoubtedly, the Cook Islands boast strong judicial precedent, which supports its asset protection legislation. There are also strong confidentiality provisions in the Cook Islands legislation, which requires government officials, trustee company and bank employees to observe strict secrecy.

But before availing yourself to the benefits of the Cook Islands trust laws, or elsewhere, you must first start with a properly structured international trust to achieve quality asset protection. We next explore how to proceed with this goal in mind.

CHAPTER FOURTEEN

How to Achieve Quality Asset Protection Planning

Creating asset protection structures for high net worth and/or high income individuals, or managing risks associated with high liability professions or occupations, has been the center of focus for me after I left behind the law practice of civil litigation and serving as a judge in civil suits. While the "asset protection" industry is still a relatively small one, I find there are many "well-intended" practitioners today putting together asset protection plans who simply don't have a clue what happens during litigation, or how to actually protect client's assets from lawsuits after a planning structure is created.

Unfortunately for the clients who fall into the hands of these "well-intended" who have put together their plans according to the latest law firm marketing guideline, their plans usually fall apart at the first threat of litigation.

The "real test" of successful asset protection planning will stand or fail in the courtroom.

I repeat: the "real test" of successful asset protection planning will stand or fail in the courtroom. Remember these words, since obtaining quality asset protection planning from top-quality experts in the field is all about achieving the desired results you seek in the *first* place.

The worst offenders are the non-attorney scam artists who put together worthless asset protection "kits" from various offshore havens. These kits don't give any real asset protection. Not only are the standard form packages generally useless, but they are rarely properly funded with the assets they are suppose to protect.

The next set of offenders are the asset protection mills churning out thousands of Family Limited Partnerships or Asset Protection Trusts at discount prices. Generally, secretaries and paralegals behind the scene crank out documents from their word processors for these operators. These planners offer no customized planning, and worse yet, they are often filled with errors and create more problems than the ones you are trying to avoid.

And too, there are the offshore service-providers who claim that their Offshore Trusts, IBCs or offshore bank accounts are "guaranteed not to fail", regardless of the problem or issue you are confronted with. These guarantees are misleading or outright false. And unfortunately, these marketing claims create a very negative image for the asset protection industry, instill doubt in the U.S. courts where they are ultimately challenged, and create unreasonable expectations by people desiring legitimate asset protection plans.

Finally, there are claims of using multiple layers of various types of entities to "secrete" assets and obtain maximum privacy. These plans are generally a waste of your time and money, and are often created for no other purpose than concealing or hiding assets. As noted earlier, the hallmark of a successful asset protection plan is *not* in hiding assets.

So then, how do you achieve quality asset protection planning in a world increasingly filled with questionable peddlers of asset protection products? The answer is to pick the right planner in the first place.

Asset protection is a legal strategy of isolating your nest egg and investments into various entities, which grow for future retirement or subsequent generations. It also means correctly managing the legal risks associated with the various type of assets and segregating "hot" or "risky" assets and activities from other non-risky types of assets or activities.

Understand that asset protection planning is *not* about guaranteeing you will never lose a dollar to a claimant or creditor. However, it is a system, or method, that ultimately should allow you to create a much stronger line of defense to resolve a dispute with far better results than if you did not have proper planning in place. Asset protection planning is, and should be, your final line of defense. You are foolhardy and simply rolling the dice if you haven't created a successful asset protection plan well in advance.

Asset protection has come to mean the integration of multi-disciplinary fields of international law and business planning for the purpose of protecting assets. Solid asset protection planning utilizes the experience of qualified and experienced multi-disciplined individuals, and reflects a high order of ethics and competence by planners in various fields using a "team approach."

Regrettably, as the field of asset protection planners has expanded in recent years, many of these well-intended planners have the skills in the *wrong* order, meaning that they have the least experience in a field where it is needed most. In other words, they are too often most experienced in the fields which are of secondary, or lesser, importance such as estate planning and taxation. While these skills are of critical importance in integrating and achieving a successful asset protection plan, they are generally totally lacking in trial and litigation skills that are needed the most to actually protect assets against lawsuits.

So then, what knowledge and experience should your asset protection planner have?

As stated above, the true test of whether asset protection planning fails or succeeds is generally in the courtroom. This is a basic premise you must remember when looking to achieve quality asset protection planning. Therefore, *first and foremost,* courtroom trial and litigation experience is essential to quality asset protection planning.

Being a seasoned and experienced trial litigator means being able to predict what judges will do when faced with your particular set of circumstances. You simply can't make reasonable trial predictions unless you have been in a number of civil trials. Attempting to predict what judges will do without understanding the courtroom and litigation tactics is akin to a "hope and a prayer." It is unfortunate how many so-called asset protection planning experts today have little or no experience in the *single most* important arena where your asset protection planning could ultimately be tested.

Second, it is essential that a planner have knowledge of the Uniform Fraudulent Transfers Act, and how your planning might be wiped out by failing to comply with this statutory law. Good asset protection plans are created through the use of corporations, partnerships, LLCs, trusts, and other like entities, and the transfer of assets into these entities. The planner must also be well-versed with the law regarding the formation, operation, and defense of these structures. And too, a good asset protection planner should be knowledgeable about bankruptcy law, since these legal tools may be needed in a time of crisis.

Third, it is important that the planners be versed in the laws of at least the main offshore jurisdictions they operate in, as well as with international banking and how monies are transferred overseas. It is no doubt that we live in an economic village today and the world is much smaller. Your planner must understand how laws and customs function from jurisdiction to jurisdiction.

Fourth, quality asset protection plans are created in coordination with competent tax professionals. It is important that no negative tax consequences be created. In the first instance, asset protection plans should be designed to be "tax neutral", meaning that they have neither positive nor negative tax consequences. At the same time, if opportunities for legal tax planning exist, this should be incorporated into the planning structure in conjunction with qualified tax professionals.

Finally, asset protection plans should be integrated with a client's estate planning. Integrating asset protection planning with estate planning is highly desirable for a variety of reasons, and allows you to achieve quality results with your planning structure. However, do not start with a planner whose first level of knowledge is estate planning and now has attempted to notch up their practice by offering asset protection on their menu.

Seek competent and experienced planners. Asset protection is like any other form of legal planning. Always hire the best attorneys who have the experience and training in the areas most important to make the plan work. Question these attorneys on what they do and how. Ask how many civil cases and courtroom trials they have successfully completed. And then, rely on their legal expertise and judgment, but always use your common sense.

For asset protection planning to work, ask yourself if you will be able to look a judge or jury in the eye and say that you are confident in what your asset protection planner has created for you. Will you be able to state that the steps you took were legal, ethical, and avoid even the appearance of impropriety?

One of the most important keys to achieving solid asset protection planning is to take steps now, well in advance of problems presenting themselves. If you wait until it is too late, then there is not much that you can do other than damage control. Take action today, while the seas are calm and before the storm sets in.

Now that you have seen how an international trust can be used for managing assets, pre-migration planning and for asset protection planning, you are better prepared for the global environment. But we haven't yet answered the questions of where and how to move your cash offshore.

CAN MY MONEY LEAVE WITH ME?

Twenty years from now you will be more disappointed by the things you didn't do than by the ones you did. So throw off the bowlines, Sail away from the safe harbor.
Catch the trade winds in your sails. Explore. Dream.
Mark Twain

CHAPTER FIFTEEN

Where Does the Money Go?

Whether it's you or your money that moves offshore, there are tax ramifications to consider *before* investing away from home. This is true regardless of your nationality, and it is particularly important if you are a U.S. citizen or tax resident.

So, before the money goes offshore, what more should you know?

By way of example, let's explore a dual U.S./UK citizen moving from the U.S. and taking up residency and domicile in the UK. What UK investments are not punitive with U.S. taxation? Can this dual national invest in UK Unit Trusts? Bank savings accounts? Money Market Funds? National Savings Certificates? Government and Corporate Bonds and shares? What does a U.S./UK investor moving to in the UK need to know?

The short answer is that a U.S. citizen (or tax resident – green card holder) who wants to avoid the PFIC (passive foreign investment company) tax and reporting obligations needs to make investments directly into individual stocks, bonds or other assets that are registered in their name. A PFIC is defined as a corporation in which 75% or more of its income is from passive investments, or where 50% or more of its assets are held to produce investment income. A savings account, a share of stock, a bond, note, certificate of deposit, life insurance policy or commercial annuity are not components of a PFIC.

In most cases, a bank money market fund or pooled income fund would be treated as a PFIC and would be subject to harsh U.S. tax treatment on the disposition of units in the fund. A hedge fund or any other kind of investment pooling arrangement where the investor is a corporation and meets the definition of a PFIC would be subject to PFIC treatment as well.

What's more, opening up a new bank account in a new venue is no longer a simple task. This is true whether you are a U.S. citizen moving to UK, or any other nationality moving to any other country. Prior to the 1990s it was easy for anyone to open a bank account worldwide.

Identification was minimal, and as long as you had money to deposit, the banks were glad to take your business.

Thanks to the OECD, FAPT and other international organizations banks were pressured to tighten up on new business in the name of fighting drugs, money laundering, and criminal activity......all loosely defined and interpreted so even the innocent fall prey.

And then came 9/11. The freedom of association and doing business around the world became even more difficult under the auspices of fighting the war on terrorism. The freedom of conducting banking business became heavily regulated and burdensome. More on international banking is covered later in another section.

Today, the biggest problem a U.S. citizen faces looking to invest offshore, in UK or elsewhere, is finding a bank that will buy foreign securities on their behalf. While it is perfectly legal, many banks outside of the U.S. are reluctant to deal with U.S. citizens, fearing a dispute with the U.S. Securities and Exchange Commission. Many U.S. investors are therefore informed by foreign brokers or banks that they will not purchase investments on their account. Instead, they require that the investments be purchased through a foreign corporation or trust.

However, even when a U.S. person buys foreign investments through a foreign corporation, that corporation then becomes a PFIC and this creates a whole new set of problems.

There are basically two ways to avoid the PFIC problem. First, is to make an election to treat the foreign corporation as a "disregarded" entity (one owner) or as a foreign partnership (more than one owner) for U.S. tax purposes. Second, is to make what is referred to as a QEF election for the foreign corporation. That has almost the same effect as the disregarded entity election.

To summarize, a U.S. citizen will need to invest directly into the asset classes, work diligently around the PFIC problem, or invest through an international trust.

Before we move on to foreign banking and other investment opportunities, you need to understand the serious ramifications of investing in foreign mutual funds ... this is a black hole to avoid if you are a U.S. citizen or tax resident.

CHAPTER SIXTEEN

Watch Out for the Foreign Mutual Fund Tax Trap

A U.S. citizen or tax resident can freely invest in mutual funds located within the U.S. However, investing in a mutual fund outside of the U.S. is a huge trap for the unwary.

In the name of protecting the innocent, U.S. mutual fund groups have lobbied to gain a huge advantage by protecting their market at home....... and in the name of the U.S. government, they are keeping a close watchful eye over all they rule.

One of the most confusing aspects of foreign investing is the difference in the treatment of foreign mutual funds as compared to U.S. based mutual funds. To understand the problem, it helps to begin with a basic explanation of the tax treatment of U.S. shareholders of a mutual fund in the U.S.

Generally, a U.S. mutual fund is treated in a manner similar to a partnership with respect to the income and the gains of the fund. The income is passed through to the shareholders in proportion to their holdings and reported to the IRS by the mutual fund. The information reported to the IRS by the mutual fund is then paired up against the reporting of the taxpayer.

Unlike with domestic mutual fund companies, the IRS is not able to keep a watchful eye over foreign investment companies or mutual funds, as they are not subject to the same kind of reporting and disclosure. And foreign companies and funds want nothing to do with the U.S. reporting burdens. Instead, the IRS places the burden on the U.S. shareholder/taxpayer to determine their share of the income of the investment company. Any type of corporate mutual fund outside the U.S. is referred to in the tax code as a PFIC (passive foreign investment company).

Without doubt, the U.S. tax laws are clearly designed to deter U.S. persons from investing in mutual funds outside the U.S. where the income or gains of the foreign funds are not subject to current taxation, as are the gains and other income of most domestic mutual funds. In addition, the tax law clearly seeks to deter U.S. persons from using a

foreign corporation as an investment fund by placing stringent requirements on these entities.

If a foreign corporation is a PFIC, the U.S. shareholders will be subject to severe tax treatment on any distributions from the PFIC unless
the PFIC elects to be subject to the SEC and the IRS reporting requirements, *or* the U.S. shareholder elects to pay tax on the undistributed current income of the PFIC (which requires the co-operation of the PFIC),
or the PFIC is listed on a national securities exchange and the shareholder elects to pay tax on any increase in the market value of the shares
from one year to the next.

All done and said, a U.S. citizen is in a far better position to invest
directly in the stock of foreign corporations not considered PFICs, or to
otherwise invest in a U.S. mutual fund that invests in foreign stocks or
foreign mutual funds.

In some cases, a U.S. person may be able to utilize a foreign variable
annuity or variable life insurance contract to invest in foreign mutual
funds, but the tax treatment will be based upon the rules for investments
in annuities or life insurance rather than for investments in the underlying stocks or mutual funds (see a discussion on this topic in a later section).

Since 1992, the United States has changed the way certain offshore
investments are taxed. The most onerous tax implication facing American
investors is the QEF rule, or Qualified Elected Fund rule. A U.S. investor
who purchases offshore mutual funds must now pay annual capital gains
from that investment even if there was no distribution. That means any
investor holding an offshore fund must pay capital gains taxes every year,
assuming he has gains, from a separate source of income. This makes offshore mutual funds a bad investment for Americans.

The bottom line is that there are huge problems associated with U.S.
citizens and tax residents investing in foreign mutual funds, which can
lead to obscene results, and where the tax and penalties can exceed the
total income and/or gains. The reason for this outlandish outcome is that
the gains from the funds are allocated to *all of the years* the fund has
been owned. Tax is then computed for each year based on the highest
rate in the tax tables – without regard to the marginal tax bracket of the
taxpayer.

To add insult to injury, a non-deductible interest charge is added to the amount of tax and compounded on a daily basis. Because gains cannot be reduced by losses, the tax and interest can easily exceed the total net gain from the investment.

Before you delve into the offshore investment world, your number one priority should be figuring out your tax situation. In other words, understand how your investments will be taxed – and which investments should be avoided – because of the harsh tax consequences found in the U.S. tax code.

Repeatedly, I've heard of numerous disaster stories where investors made offshore investments through a foreign bank account, but didn't bother to check out the tax consequences *before* investing. Later, they were shocked when they were hit hard by punitive taxes.

International stocks are a different story altogether. If you choose to buy foreign stocks, either domestically or from a private bank abroad, then make sure you buy these securities in a taxable account so you can reclaim the dividend withholding at source.

Foreign bonds also pose a similar dilemma to some retirement investors. If you buy international bonds in an IRA or in any other tax-deferred account, interest income will be withheld. And because you cannot reclaim a credit in a retirement plan, you'll lose a portion of the income, a bad result since interest-income is a big part of a bond's total return. But you can claim that withholding outside of a retirement plan.

Going global with even a portion of your investment portfolio can yield some impressive long-term results, in addition to risk management. But make sure you fully understand the tax implications of investing in foreign securities before investing.

But what of opening and depositing your money into a foreign bank?

CHAPTER SEVENTEEN

Bank Accounts & Foreign Banking

From time to time someone who hasn't traveled, lived or invested outside of their homeland asks me whether it is legal to open a foreign bank account. They have fears of government agents breaking down the doors at night and treating them like common criminals. Those that have banked with "offshore" financial institutions understand the process can be different than at home.

The short answer is that it is perfectly legal for most global citizens to maintain a foreign bank account, including U.S. persons. In particular, however, the U.S. government wants to know about those accounts primarily for tax reporting reasons.

U.S. citizens and permanent residents are required by law to report any income from foreign bank accounts. Even though the income earned in those accounts is not reported to the IRS, it does not alter the legal requirement of a U.S. citizen or tax resident.

Furthermore, a foreign bank account is also required to be disclosed on Tax Form 1040 when your personal return is filed, and again on Form TDF 90-22.1 by June 30th to disclose the bank and other information about all foreign accounts, when the aggregate of all accounts is greater than $10,000 at any time during the prior calendar year. There are severe penalties for a willful failure to file Form TDF 90-22.1.

The IRS has sold the U.S. Congress that many U.S. citizens are evading taxes by going "offshore" with their banking, trusts and corporations. The IRS's mission is to discover every dime of unreported income, regardless of the price of enforcement.

I have serious doubts that the practice is as widespread as the IRS and other tax authorities argue, but that is their position. I certainly do not see evidence of this from my clients.

Keep in mind that if you are a tax evader, there is no statute of limitations on auditing your tax return. If in the retirement years the authorities find out about a foreign bank account you forgot to tell them about, it's all subject to penalties and interest plus the taxes, regardless of how long it took to become uncovered.

Further, U.S. tax evasion has no dollar threshold.

And how do the IRS and other tax authorities catch tax evaders using offshore bank accounts?

First, it is almost impossible to transfer money of any value offshore without leaving a paper trail. Even if you legally transfer under the threshold amount of $10,000 in currency offshore, it would take a long time, and not be cost effective, to build a hidden nest egg. And even if you went down this slow route, a bank employee is likely to file a suspicious activity report on you for so many cash transactions. Basically, you would have to engage in a lot of very small transfers of money, spread out over many years, in order to avoid leaving a trail.

And too, transfers of large amounts of cash leaves an electronic, if not a paper trail. An auditor's job is to find things that don't fit a pattern. Passive income is down, deposits are missing, money ratios don't fit, or financial trends change for no apparent reason. Most tax agents are well-trained in their craft as auditors.

Good auditors are like detectives. They acquire a sixth sense when things don't look right. They sense when someone is lying or is nervous. They know how to observe body language and sense when a taxpayer might be trying to hide something. The more of these clues they get, the more they want to get to the bottom of things. Do something wrong, and they can become your worst enemy.

And too, if things don't add up, a tax agent can perform a lifestyle audit. Instead of just looking at your tax returns and supporting records, they look into every nook and cranny of your personal life for clues to unreported income. They then try to reconstruct how much income you would need to support a particular lifestyle. If you haven't reported that much income, they dig deeper.

Don't gamble on winning the audit "lottery" … your return might be one of the random numbers they pull for this year. And too, there is always the risk of being reported for tax evasion by someone you know. Someone you bragged to one too many times, an ex-partner or ex-spouse, former business partner, or disgruntled employee.

Today many foreign banks don't want anything to do with U.S. account holders in particular, unless there is substantial balance of

$100,000 or more. If the account holder lives outside the U.S. this is often relaxed. And some foreign banks require much larger deposits to take on new accounts with a U.S. citizen. There is simply too much profitable banking business available today without banks taking on the headaches associated with U.S. citizens and the cross they bear........ compliments of Uncle Sam.

These are the facts of life in offshore banking today with respect to U.S. and most other nationals. So this means it will take time, effort and money to build a new relationship with a foreign bank. Be prepared to fill out papers and reams of forms as your banker performs his or her due diligence and gets to know his new customer. The good old days of depositing large amounts of cash, with no questions asked, are long gone.

Even with the above being said, there has been a huge global shift away from the U.S. as a major money center. Because of this shift, it is increasingly important to learn how to manage offshore bankers and understand the culture they work in today.

And keep in mind offshore banking centers are changing.

CHAPTER EIGHTEEN

Offshore Investing

New York has long been seen as the world's investment capital. But now, New York risks losing its status as the world's primary financial center to fast-developing cities like Hong Kong, and so acknowledges New York City mayor Michael Bloomberg.

Bloomberg said in a press conference recently that New York is losing ground to centers like Hong Kong and London as they become leaders in capital formation. He believes more money will be raised through initial public offerings (IPOs) in Hong Kong than in either London or New York.

Mr. Bloomberg was quoted as saying that "New York cannot ignore these warning signs. Unless we improve our corporate climate, we risk allowing New York to lose its pre-eminence in the global financial services sector. This would be devastating for both our city and nation."

Unfortunately for the U.S., the transition has started long ago and it is probably much too late for a turnaround anytime soon. For political, economic and philosophical reasons, investors worldwide are moving their money elsewhere. Money always goes to where it is treated best.

Nonetheless, the U.S. mayor has hired a consulting firm to create an "action plan" for the New York financial sector. The firm will issue a report identifying which factors are keeping New York at a competitive disadvantage, but you need look no further than the Hong Kong financial center.

Hong Kong-based analysts cited high regulatory costs and litigation threats as disadvantages to New York stock listings. In the future, they claim, most Chinese firms seeking overseas listing will prefer Hong Kong, after China Life and Bank of China (Hong Kong) listed in New York and were met by lawsuits from U.S. investors demanding more information disclosure.

Mr. Bloomberg stated four factors are responsible for the threat to New York. These are:

- Globalization of capital markets

- Overregulation

- Frivolous litigation

- Incompatible accounting standards

True, but unfortunately Mr. Bloomberg is already behind the curve. Americans are only now beginning to realize "there appears to be a worrying trend of corporate leaders focusing inordinate time on compliance minutiae rather than innovative strategies for growth, for fear of facing personal financial penalties from overzealous regulators."

This change, which Bloomberg and the business leaders are only now recognizing actually began in the 1960s as the consumer rights movements began to take place. The shift from "buyer beware" to "somebody has to take blame" in the 1970s and 1980s lead to an all out litigation frenzy during the 1980's and the 1990s. Smart money has been looking globally during the past decade or more.

Since the mid-1990s, overseas companies with regional operations in Hong Kong have increased by over 50 per cent. At the end of Q-3 2006, 1,152 companies were listed on the Hong Kong bourse of which 352 were mainland companies. These firms account for 44 per cent of total market capitalization and supply about 57 per cent of daily turnover.

By the end of 2006, Hong Kong ranked number one in the world for total capital raised by means of IPOs. Indeed, the recent IPO of ICBC (Industrial and Commercial Bank of China) in Hong Kong raised US$20 billion, a new worldwide record.

If you don't recognize the shift for smart money to new ports of call, you too are missing the boat.

A popular reason for investing offshore is to gain access to foreign investments. Whether you are moving outside your homeland or seeking asset protection through foreign entities, you will need to continue to grow your understanding of how the financial markets operate outside your home base. Often times this will push you beyond your comfort zone, but this is all part of the learning process. It would be impossible to list all of the financial factors you need to consider in any one country, let alone in multiple jurisdictions. For illustrative purposes, we will continue to explore what a U.S. person should consider when investing some of their assets offshore.

Of particular importance, there are numerous special tax rules found in U.S. tax law intended to deter U.S. investors from venturing outside the U.S. in order to reduce or defer their taxes. The most onerous of these rules is the tax treatment of foreign mutual funds owned by U.S. taxpayers as discussed earlier.

As covered in more detail above, if a foreign corporation is a passive foreign investment company (a PFIC), then U.S. shareholders are subject to a very punitive tax on accumulated distributions from the fund or from gains on the disposition of shares of the fund. One way to avoid the punitive tax is if the foreign fund is willing to disclose substantial financial information, then the punitive tax can be avoided by making an election to pay taxes on the shareholder's portion of the current income of the fund. Another way to avoid the punitive test is to elect to pay taxes on the gain in the market value of the fund each year, otherwise referred to as the "mark to market" election. This election is only available to U.S. shareholders of foreign funds that can be bought and sold through a major national auction market similar to the New York Stock Exchange.

U.S. persons who want to invest in foreign hedge funds are therefore limited to those that are organized as partnerships or are controlled by U.S. investors. Alternatively, you can invest in a foreign variable annuity or foreign variable life insurance policy that invests in a hedge fund.

Many U.S. investors looking to invest in companies generally invest directly in their stocks, due to the burdens they encounter with foreign mutual funds. The bottom line is that the U.S. Securities and Exchange Commission (SEC) makes it very difficult and costly for foreign companies or brokers (and banks) to sell their stocks or bonds to U.S. persons. Most foreign financial institutions and companies simply do not want to hassle with the costly U.S. regulatory process, so they refuse to sell to U.S. citizens. Often times they won't even respond to an inquiry from a U.S. person.

But there is an alternative. U.S. investors can gain access to a much broader foreign investment market if they purchase indirectly through a foreign trustee, a foreign corporation or a foreign limited liability company. This has led many U.S. investors to form a foreign corporation or foreign trust in a tax haven country in order to invest in foreign securities.

But beware, since this brings about a new set of problems.

First, a U.S. grantor on his behalf and his U.S. beneficiaries of a foreign trust (the foreign tax type trust, not the type we recommend), is required to file Form 3520 each year they have any transactions with the trust. The trustee of the foreign trust must also file Form 3520-A. Failure to comply with these requirements are heavy, and penalties are assessed against the U.S. grantor.

Second, if a U.S. investor uses a foreign corporation to acquire foreign securities, the taxpayer must file Form 5471 each year for shareholders of certain foreign corporations. This results in passing certain (subpart F) income of the corporation to some of the U.S. shareholders and it eliminates the tax benefit of any capital gains or dividend income. Even if the foreign corporation is owned by a foreign trust, the trust grantor is treated as the owner of the assets in the trust for tax purposes, and the trust is therefore transparent and the trust grantor must still file the Form 5471.

One way to avoid some of these problems is to form a foreign limited liability company (LLC) or eligible foreign corporation referred to as an international business corporation (IBC). An election can then be made for the LLC or IBC to be treated as a disregarded entity for tax purposes. If the foreign LLC or IBC has more than one owner it will be treated as a foreign partnership and a Form 8865 must be filed. If the foreign LLC or IBC has only one owner, it will be totally disregarded for tax purposes and the owner of the LLC or IBC will personally report income and expenses of the LLC or IBC. And too, a disregarded entity is required to file a Form 8858 each year, which is attached to the tax return of the owner of the entity.

As noted earlier, U.S. persons who have $10,000 or more in any combination of foreign financial accounts at any time during the tax year must also file a Form TDF 90-22.1 with the Treasury Department on or before June 30th of the following year. Filing this report at the same time you file your personal tax returns is a good habit to get into so it is not forgotten come June. An acknowledgement of the foreign account must also be stated in your personal tax return.

As you shift your investments outside of your homeland jurisdiction, you have a choice of holding your money in your local or in a foreign currency. This presents another set of issues as you consider the relative value of currencies in relation to one another, and creating profits or losses separate from the underlying investment.

CHAPTER NINETEEN

The World of Foreign Currencies

From the beginning, gold was the currency we traded in which held value. Long before our generation gold was the currency of exchange for goods and services.

Then things changed. During this past century "fiat" currencies issued by governments have taken the place of gold. Whether gold should be in your portfolio, is a decision for you alone to make. Today, foreign exchange in currencies is how international trade occurs. If you take up residency somewhere new, you will need to acquire the local currencies to live and do business in that country. A pocket full of gold coins won't get you very far.

The gains and losses when a currency exchange occurs for citizens around the world are basically the same, but we will only comment on how U.S. citizens and residents will be taxed when they cross over with cash from one currency to another and the gain they realize from the profit from the trade. Today the U.S. Dollar is the leading currency worldwide, but that is changing soon.

But first, consider how we made the transition from the gold standard to fiat currencies. This helps to understand how we arrived to our present situation.

Gold has served as money in all great civilizations throughout history, first coined more than 2,500 years ago in Mesopotamia. However, it is the change in the status of *how* we view gold today that figures significantly in our lives.

Monetary fraud began in 1914, when Congress created The Federal Reserve and gave the Fed unlimited ability to issue dollars. At the time dollars still carried the statement *"Payable to the Bearer in Gold Coin."*

A vast expansion of the currency ensued, leading to the boom of the "roaring twenties", and ultimately to the crash of 1929. Dollar holders, fearing banks were in trouble, began demanding the gold they had been promised. The banks didn't have enough gold, and the bankruptcies began.

In the early 1930s, between US$90 billion and US$125 billion in bonds were held in the U.S. Each bond promised to pay in gold to their holders to protect them from currency depreciation. One of the issuers of such bonds was the Iron Mountain Railroad – later part of the Missouri Pacific. In 1902 it floated a 30-year bond issue with the promise to repay the bonds at maturity in U. S. gold coin "of the present standard of weight and fineness." In May 1933 when the bonds were due, Manhattan's Bankers Trust, owner of the bonds, demanded payment in gold.

The railroad refused and Bankers Trust sued. Federal Judge Charles Breckenridge Faris in that case concluded that if the gold clause was held *literally* binding, $1,693 devalued dollars would have to be paid on each $1,000 bond. In his words *"it would bankrupt well nigh every railroad, every municipality . . . and well nigh every State in the union. Congress alone has power to say what shall be used as money"*, concluded Judge Faris, and *"the gold clause is therefore unenforceable."* The very thing lenders feared would happen, did occur: they had been cheated by currency depreciation.

Politicians came to the rescue. In 1933, President Roosevelt declared a bank holiday, suspended gold payments, and made it illegal for Americans to own or make contracts in gold. Congress passed legislation knocking the gold clause out of every U. S. bond, public and private. It was this legislation that Judge Feris upheld.

Then, as the end of World War II was still raging, the Bretton Woods Agreement emerged and the U.S. currency was pegged as the "world currency" and set the value of all other currencies globally. After pressure fell on the U.S. Dollar during the 1970s, President Nixon made it legal to privately own gold again.

In 1985, the G5 countries (U.S., Japan, Germany, France and the UK) met at the Plaza Hotel in New York City and an important agreement was reached called the Plaza Accord. Basically the agreement called for a controlled devaluation of the U.S. Dollar against the German mark and the Japanese yen. The reason was simple: to reduce America's ballooning current account deficit.

Since 1985, gold reserves and values have fluctuated widely …. and if history is any guide, this pattern will continue. It looks like another international currency agreement may be in the works. This time the U.S. Dollar may be devalued against the Chinese Yuan – for much the same reason as in 1985: America's runaway current account deficit.

What is important to understand is that the value of gold and the U.S. Dollar have historically moved in an inverse relationship as investors look for a hedge against a failing dollar. As a result, the "gold bugs" believe that a certain amount of this tangible currency belongs in all of our portfolios, while other investors are less inclined. This choice is for you to make.

The argument for gold is that it is a real, tangible good. It can't be created out of thin air or with the stroke of a computer key, as dollars are created. Relative to the U.S. dollar, gold is not just a bargain, it is the sovereign individual's ultimate hedge against fiat money. Therefore, as the argument goes, we should own it as a commodity, own the shares of companies that produce it, and find ways to trade it and make our contracts in it.

However, the other side of the argument is that gold today is nothing more than an investment hedge against the U.S. Dollar. Another investment choice in a diversified portfolio, it is said. In reality, the value of gold against other currencies globally (i.e. other than the US$) has seen little, if any, appreciation and other international investment choices yield far better returns.

Naturally, if you include gold in your investment portfolio and sell it for a profit, you need to report the gain for tax purposes. This is also true for global currencies, as you move your money in and out of different currencies against the U.S. Dollar or other currency.

The primary source of information on the tax treatment of currency gains or losses for U.S. persons is found in the Internal Revenue Code Section 988.

The general rule with regard to the U.S. tax treatment of gains or losses from exchanging U.S. currency for non U.S. currency – and back again – is that the gain or loss on the currency exchange will be taxed the same as the underlying transaction. The *Taxpayer's Relief Act of 1997* included a provision in Section 1104(a) that included some changes in dealing with currency exchanges.

Under the Act, where there are currency gains or losses in connection with a trade or business or with the management or administration of investment assets, the gain is treated as an *ordinary gain* and any loss is generally treated as an expense. Particular attention should be made that the trade is not treated as a capital gain.

However, where currency gains or losses are incurred in connection with the purchase of an investment, the gain or loss on the currency change when selling the currency is a capital gain or loss and is included as part of the total capital gain or loss on the investment.

Currency gains of $200 or less that arise from personal transactions, other than for investment or business, are not taxable, but personal currency losses are not deductible. A personal transaction includes any gain or loss arising from travel even if the travel is business related. Any currency gains in excess of $200 per transaction (per trip or per purchase) are treated as a capital gain. Losses on currency exchanges for business travel are generally not deductible.

Sounds simple..... right?

Before you jump in and transfer your cash holdings from one currency to another, be aware that there are trends in the relative value of one currency against another. The traded weighted index – the value of a currency against a "basket" of commonly traded currencies – varies over time and goes up and down in a cyclical fashion. Most so called currency experts agree that the U.S. has been in a bear market (down cycle) since 2002, and may continue downward in the short term. If history is a teacher, then like all cycles, when the value of the US$ hits bottom, it will begin its climb upwards in value.

It's always difficult to pinpoint where we are in terms of a trend. Are things likely to continue downward, stay flat, or start a fresh trend upward? Long-term trends in the currency markets have historically averaged six to ten years. Dollar trends have been measured by the various bull and bear markets even long before President Nixon made the dollar a free-floating currency market in 1971.

Here is an example of long-term bear and bull markets in the dollar as measured by the US$ Index since 1971:

- 1971-1978: Seven-year bear market (President Nixon allowed the US$ to free float and the gold window closed)

- 1978-1985: Six-year bull market (Fed Chairman Volcker tightens up on inflation)

- 1985-1992: Seven-year bear market (Triggered by the Plaza Accord)

- 1992-2002: Ten-year bull market (Tech boom and increase in money supply worldwide)

- 2002- ? : The US$ continues in a bear market

No one can say for sure when the current bear market in the US$ will end. However, what astute investors do is keep these price movements in perspective to better evaluate conditions as they develop that may indicate the potential for a change in the trend.

And there are identifiable "waves" within a trend based on human emotion and generally supported by underlying economic fundamentals at various stages. Below is an example of phases in a trend as a currency goes through stages in a boom/bust price cycle...

- **Phase 1: An Unrecognized Trend** – This is early in a cycle and represents the beginning of a new trend.... key players in the market work hard to identify this stage to get on board early as cycles are about to shift in a new direction.

- **Phase 2: A Self-Perpetuating Movement** – This is the stage where the consensus (or everyday investors) begin to realize that underlying fundamentals are moving the market..... it is often the most powerful and longest leg or wave of the trend.

- **Phase 3: Testing the Trend** – There is often a pull-back that challenges new levels and the consensus' view as to the direction of a proposed trend. It can sometimes represent a significant retrace of the prior wave.

- **Phase 4: Reinforcing Expectations vs. Testing Reality** – This is the last major step in a trend. The level supported by fundamentals is challenged by expectations. It also represents the stage in which the currency is either overvalued" or "undervalued" on a pure fundamental basis.

- **Phase 5: The End is Near** – This is the stage in the cycle where some currency investors begin to realize the currency cannot be supported by the fundamentals, and get ready to move on to other currencies for their profits.

- **Phase 6: The Peak** – The final stage. The end of the road. It also generally represents an "overshoot" of the cycle we often see in currency markets due to sentiment driven and over zealous market participants.

- **Phase 7: A New Cycle is Born** – The cycle is completed and a trend begins in the opposite direction.

The above information on currency cycles is not intended to encourage you to trade in currencies. However, you should be aware of cycles and consider the different phases when you are considering when it is the right time to transfer funds into another currency.

Using New Zealand currency as an example, in late 2001 NZ$ against the US$ was around .3900.... historical lows. This meant it took .39 U.S. Dollars to buy one Kiwi Dollar. In early 2006 it was at historical highs around .70, and again in April 2007 the conversion rate hovered around .74 due to the carry trade (i.e. borrowing low in one currency and investing into currencies yielding higher interest rates).

Knowing that the NZ$ as measured against the US$ was still in its historical high range, if you didn't need to buy NZ$, why not wait until it fell closer to .50 or .55 and receive more NZ$ for your currency?

Unfortunately, there is a huge class of global investors that don't understand the above concept.

Japanese and European investors with myopic vision chased higher yields offered by financial institutions during 2006 at 7.5% on cash deposits as they supported the carry trade. The so-called experts sold these poor Mom and Pop investors NZ$ bonds with high yields, but failed to properly educate them that they stood to lose a significant portion of their principal if, and when, the NZ$ gets staged to fall, wiping out their interest rate gains..... and much more.

So whether you buy a currency for reasons of investment or due to a move to another country, take the time to understand the relative value of the currency in relation to its highs and lows. You might not be able to peg the movement of the trend "right on", but at least you are able to make a better informed decision before changing currencies.

One of the challenging aspects of the above in future years is how the demographics of our aging baby-boomers will come into play and affect currency values worldwide. Movements and swings could very well be exaggerated, if for no other reason than the power of their sheer numbers. I believe globally we are going to see some very interesting swings around the world in investments as baby-boomers start their retirement.

So where is the U.S. Dollar bear market as I write this today in mid 2007? I am absolutely certain of only one thing … it will do "something" as the cycle moves forward.

It seems some investors are acting like there is no end in sight to better times (Phase 2). Other big players have been testing the market for the highs and lows (Phase 3), while the savvy investors are testing the fundamentals (Phase 4). I personally think we have pasted through Phase 4 and believe the end is already is sight for the U.S. Dollar (Phase 5). It is possible that some will still make money in the currencies with US$ if they get out "just in time" before the peak (Phase 6), but most will be left without a chair to sit in when the music stops and we begin a shift towards a new trend (Phase 7). On this fundamental basis – at this stage today – it appears the Euro and Pound are "overvalued" against the dollar. But, there are probably some goods reasons why it makes sense to be short the dollar, since this bear market has only been going on for 5 years. If your crystal ball offers a clearer perspective, please email me and let me know at Datlegal@aol.com

We are always brilliant looking backwards… the trick is trying to have an insight into what the future brings as currencies and other asset classes go through their cycles.

With so much else to consider in going offshore, it is amazing we have time left over to get things right and keep up with reporting legal and tax requirements. But getting things right is critical to avoid the headaches that can follow if we are derelict in our duties. Before I overwhelm U.S. readers with the tax reporting and compliances matters, we will look at the largest, wealthiest, most popular tax haven in the world, of which may surprise you.

TAXES & EXPATS: UNCLE SAM WANTS YOU!

*No government should be without censor and where the
press is free, no one ever will.*
Thomas Jefferson

CHAPTER TWENTY

When You Go Global, Get it Right

Recent IRS data confirms that the US. tax burden, contrary to popular myth, is disproportionately borne by the wealthiest taxpayers. Ranked by income for 2005, the top 1% of tax filers paid 36.9% of all personal income taxes. The average tax rate for the top 1% was 23.5%. The top 10% accounted for 68.2% of all taxes paid. Even more relevant is that the top half of all taxpayers paid 96.7% of all personal income taxes. The next time someone comments that tax cuts only affect the wealthiest half of taxpayers, point out that this same group are the ones that pay 96.7% of the taxes in the first place!

Do you want some mind-numbing numbers that concern the damnable U.S. income tax system? Here are some sickening statistics.

By the U.S. government's own estimates it takes an average U.S. taxpayer 28 hours and 30 minutes to complete a 1040 tax return – 42 minutes longer than last year. And 60% of all taxpayers need paid professional help in order to file their taxes.

What's more, according to the Government Accounting Office (GAO), individuals and businesses spend 5 billion hours annually complying with the income tax. Estimated annual compliance costs are over $200 billion – more than it costs to produce every U.S. car, truck and van. In 2000, individual income taxes consumed 10.2% of the entire U.S. GDP.

When the first national income tax became law in 1913, the entire Internal Revenue Code (IRC) fit into 173 pages. Today? Well, the IRC contains over 60,000 pages and there are nearly 500 IRS forms, each with many pages of fine print instructions and schedules to be attached.

What's more, the IRS publishes and distributes over 8 billion pages of forms and notices each year which – if laid end to end – would circle the earth 28 times… imagine that!

Admittedly, the tax code is so complex even the IRS can't figure it out. A U.S. Treasury investigation found that IRS employees gave the wrong answer about 50% of the time in response to taxpayers' questions.

If you flipped a coin, your chances would be just as accurate as contacting the IRS help line and you wouldn't have to listen to the automated telephone options and wait in a queue for 40 minutes.

And then the GAO reported that in auditing 45 random IRS transactions, 16 were properly calculated and 29 were wrong, an error rate of 64%! Don't believe me? Look at GAO Pub. 94-120.

And still more: the administrative costs for the grossly over-bloated 114,000 employee IRS bureaucracy alone exceeds $10 billion a year. That number is five times the number of FBI agents and twice as many as CIA employees.

For sure, government bureaucrats with all the answers are best suited to regulate the American way of life...... right, and I am Caesar!

After reviewing some of the tax reporting and compliance requirements for U.S. citizens you are by now probably very frustrated... welcome to the club. Misery loves company.

To make matters worse, the international section of the tax law is the most difficult and grossly convoluted of any section of the tax code. For that reason, the comments and references to some of the rules in this book are therefore over-simplified, and as a result, excessive simplification can cause inaccuracy and misleading information.

You might be surprised to know the IRS is not the main culprit in terms of the complexity of our tax laws. Your anger or frustration should be directed at the Senators and Congressmen who serve on the tax committees of Congress. They write the absurd language into the laws the IRS is required to administer. The IRS then takes this complex legislation and prepares insanely confusing regulations that supposedly "interpret" the laws. The result is a need for a translator to understand the so-called "interpretation" by the IRS. Confusion, frustration and insanity are words that come to my mind.

As you take your investments global, it's important to understand the potential drawbacks – especially if you are a U.S. citizen or tax resident.

Take something as simple as purchasing a vacation home in another country. Expenses for the property will be denominated in the local currency, so it makes sense to open a bank account locally to pay them, and also to receive any rental income if you rent it out.

By merely opening the bank account, you have started a compliance process you need to follow. As noted earlier, if the value of all offshore accounts you have signature or other authority over exceeds US$10,000 at any time during the year, you must report this to the IRS on your federal income tax return *and* to the U.S. Treasury on Form TDF 90-22.1. Failure to report the account on both forms, each year, can result in a five-year prison sentence and a US$500,000 fine...a huge price to pay for what is in most cases an innocent omission. The reporting is simple and easy, but don't forget it.

Similar compliance requirements exist if a U.S. citizen purchases the vacation home through a foreign corporation. This is perfectly legal, but you must report any transfer of assets to the foreign corporation on IRS Form 926 and submit a detailed annual reporting form to the IRS each year on Form 5471.

All of this reporting to keep Uncle Sam happy as you lounge poolside offshore.

And whether you hail to the flag of the U.S., U.K., E.U., N.Z., Australia, Canada or elsewhere, there are other issues to be aware of in the country where you purchase the vacation home.

For example, you may find yourself liable to inheritance tax or probate proceedings in that country at the death of a co-owner. Numerous solutions are available to avoid this problem, but you must plan for this in advance. In Canada – for example – a married couple can structure the purchase of Canadian property through a U.S. trust. At the death of one spouse, the other will inherit without it being subject to Canadian probate proceedings.

The burdens fall not only in your homeland, but in the country where your investments are held.

The above is only the beginning. Even though I am routinely involved in dealing with tax issues as an aside with the experts, I am not a tax "expert" and rely upon the expertise of others for whom I respect. As a practical matter, the purpose of the tax comments are therefore to provide an overview and simply to warn you that there are numerous pitfalls to be aware of when investing outside your homeland.

Whatever you do, don't let the compliance and regulatory provisions of your home country or foreign venues scare you off. Just make sure you get good professional advice *before* taking the plunge. Good off-shore pre-migration planning is essential (and not *just* before).

Ever wonder where the biggest tax haven in the world is located? Read on to find out.

CHAPTER TWENTY ONE

The Biggest Tax Haven in the World?
You May be Surprised

Do you know where the largest tax haven of the world is located? Is it in the Caribbean? The South Pacific? The Middle East or in Asia? Most people are surprised when they learn.

The answer is that the USA is the largest tax haven for the rest of the world – and a huge tax haven it is…. but not for U.S. citizens or permanent residents.

Citizens and residents living in high tax countries *other than* the U.S. are generally subject to income taxes on investments anywhere in the world as long as those investments are owned directly. However, in many countries the income earned by assets held by a foreign trust or foreign corporation are not subject to tax in the resident country. If the trust or corporation is located in a tax haven jurisdiction, the income from those assets and investments may legally avoid taxes entirely. Unfortunately, this does not apply to U.S. citizens.

U.S. Citizens and permanent residents are subject to tax on their worldwide income. This draconian and overly burdensome U.S. tax law is unique in the world and surpasses all others.

To the contrary, a *non-resident* investor in the U.S. is only subject to U.S. tax on certain U.S. source income. Many sources of U.S. income from investments are tax exempt for a non-resident investor in the U.S.

The citizens of other countries who do not reside in the U.S. for more than 183 days in a single year, or more than an average of 120 days per year, and who do not have a "green card" permitting them to live and work in the U.S. indefinitely, can invest in an assortment of U.S. securities on a tax-favored basis. This is what makes the U.S. the largest tax haven in the world.

Basically, a non-resident investor can invest in the bonds of the U.S. government or the debt obligations of U.S. banks and most other financial institutions on a tax-free basis. They may be subject to tax in their own country, but not in the U.S. The interest on U.S. corporate bonds may also be exempt from U.S. tax if the bonds are purchased by non-residents and non-citizens of the U.S.

In addition, a non-resident investor who realizes a gain on the sale of stocks or bonds in U.S. securities is not subject to any capital gains tax. This is another big plus for foreign investors.

What's more, the U.S. has virtually no income tax reporting requirement to foreign countries, allowing foreign investors to independently report income, or not. Congress has specially declined income reporting requirements to foreign countries for foreign investors out of fear of a mass-exodus of investment funds.

Naturally, many U.S. citizens or permanent residents would like to become a non-resident investor and enjoy these outstanding tax advantages. As a result, the U.S. tax law is designed to prevent tax avoidance for U.S. citizens through the use of intermediate foreign entities, such as LLCs, FLPs and IBCs. To enjoy the tax advantage of a non-resident investor, the U.S. person must first become an expatriate and relinquish his or her U.S. citizenship or resident status. But for those individuals seeking this path, there are complex rules designed to ensure that any unrealized gains from tax deferred investments are subject to U.S. taxation.

Basically, the only taxes foreign investors are obligated to pay are on dividends on U.S. stocks or U.S. real estate.

Dividends on U.S. stocks are subject to tax by a non-resident investor and are subject to a withholding rate of 30%. However, if the U.S. has a treaty with the foreign country in which the non-resident investor is a resident, the rate of withholding may be less.

And if a non-resident investor purchases U.S. real estate, there is a 10% withholding tax that must be withheld by the seller when the property is sold. If the actual tax is less than the withholding tax, the non-resident investor can file a U.S. income tax return to obtain a refund of any excess withholding.

The tax benefits are pretty substantial for a non-resident investor. Very interesting how the U.S. government caters to foreign investors offering outstanding tax benefits to stimulate foreign investment within, but stigmatizes any other country offering U.S. citizens even a paltry equivalent for investments offshore.

Don't grow weary of the tax issues just yet, because next we discuss a selection of tax reporting requirements for foreign investors and U.S. persons going offshore. Better you discover them now than learn later, the hard way.

CHAPTER TWENTY TWO

International Tax Returns & You

Whether as a foreign investor investing in the U.S., or as a U.S. person investing offshore, tax reporting obligations arise under various circumstances. Again, what follows is a brief summary from what I have seen in dealing with the experts that prepare tax returns for international investors, living on both sides of the pond.

For example, if foreign investors are employed in the U.S. on a temporary basis, they are subject to the same payroll tax withholdings as a U.S. person. They are also generally subject to U.S. Social Security taxes on their earned income. However, the allowable exemptions and deductions are different from a U.S. taxpayer at tax time.

The same is also true if the non-resident investor is engaged in a trade or business in the U.S. In this case they are subject to U.S. tax on that income, but with different rules for the allowable exemptions and deductions that may be claimed.

A corporation or partnership that is not domiciled in the U.S. but which has a U.S. employee, agent or other 'substantial presence' is generally subject to U.S. tax on the U.S. source income, but not on their foreign source income. A non-resident investor may also be subject to U.S. estate or gift taxes on certain U.S. based assets, and they are not permitted the same exemption as a U.S. citizen or resident.

From a U.S. citizen's perspective, the IRS has devoted significant attention to the imposition and collection of penalties for late filing of various tax or information returns for international investors.

In many cases, penalties require far less time and effort than an IRS audit, since they are usually based on simple fact situations. For example, was an income tax return or information return required by IRS regulations? If so, was it filed on time? Was any tax due? If so, was it fully paid and on time?

An example of aggressive IRS penalty tactics was a $95,000 penalty that was assessed for allegedly filing a return six days late. In 2005, a timely filed return was sent to the IRS for a foreign trust due on March

15. The IRS claimed they did not get the form until March 21st and an IRS agent imposed a penalty of 5% of the assets in the trust, amounting to a $95,000 penalty. In this case the tax preparer mailed the client's return for the client through the U.S. postal service with a certified mail receipt. However, because the IRS failed to retain a copy of the mailing envelope with the mailing date, the mailing date couldn't be established, and the penalty was eventually dropped. Only after significant efforts by the taxpayer and the tax preparer was the $95,000 penalty rescinded.

According to most tax preparers, as a general rule, individual income tax return Form 1040 does not have to be filed if no tax is due based upon the amount of income and statutory deductions or exemptions. Otherwise, there is a penalty of between 5% and 25% of the tax due for each month the return is filed late. The corporate income tax return Form 1120 is required to be filed regardless of whether a tax is due, with the same penalty for late filing, but only if there is a tax amount.

With the exception of the above, for all other tax and information returns, there is a specific penalty for a failure to file the form or for late filing – *regardless of whether any additional tax is due.* The reason for this harsh result is simply because the information is required to be reported.

Filing late can result in punitive financial penalties, but rarely criminal charges. Not filing and getting caught can result in criminal prosecution. And beware, consultation with an accountant is not protected as a privileged communication as is a consultation with an attorney. Although an attorney *cannot* advise a client that it is best not to file a return or a form, the attorney cannot be compelled to testify as to the nature of the consultation. However, an accountant or other tax preparer *can* be compelled to testify. So if a taxpayer discusses the matter with an accountant and then decides not to file, the accountant could be compelled to disclose the details of the discussion.

The best opportunity for confidentiality is therefore to retain an attorney who then hires the accountant to discuss tax matters on your behalf.

Do you think that hiding income is a hallmark of quality tax planning? Think again.

There are many ways the IRS could discover taxpayer fraud or income tax evasion. It is always possible for the IRS to uncover information indirectly from various sources, regarding the existence of unreported foreign bank or other financial accounts, foreign credit cards, foreign trusts or foreign corporations. That is likely to lead to an audit, which in turn could easily result in producing information that the taxpayer thought was well-concealed.

The Congress and the IRS have become particularly frustrated by the failure of certain U.S. taxpayers to file the information returns required for foreign trusts, foreign corporations, foreign partnerships, foreign disregarded entities, foreign mutual funds and other foreign financial accounts. As a result, heavy penalties have been imposed for these types of entities. What follows are some of the filing requirements.

For example, a Form 3520-A is required annually for a Foreign Trust (for U.S. tax purposes) with a U.S. Grantor (but not for U.S. domestic grantor trusts used for offshore and international trusts of the type our office generally recommends). A penalty of 5% of the gross value of the portion of the trust assets may result if the U.S. grantor of the foreign trust fails to file a timely Form 3520-A or does not provide the information required. An extension of time to file can be requested with Form 2758.

A Form 3520 is required annually to Report Transactions with Foreign Trusts and Foreign Gifts (again, not required for U.S. domestic grantor trusts used for offshore and international trust purposes). The penalties for a failure to file this form includes (1) 35% of the gross value of the distributions received from a foreign trust or transferred to a foreign trust, and (2) 5% per month for the amount of certain foreign gifts (with a maximum of 25%). Penalties may be waived by the IRS on a showing of reasonable cause for a failure to file. This form is due with the income tax return of the U.S. grantor of the foreign trust, including any extensions of time to file.

A Form 5471 is required of U.S. Persons with respect to certain Foreign Corporations. This is due with the income tax return of the U.S. shareholder, officer or director of a foreign corporation. The $10,000 penalty for failing to file this form is severe, even though no tax may be due. The penalties may be waived by the IRS on a showing of reasonable cause for failing to file the form. However, if the taxpayer is notified by the IRS of a duty to file, the penalty is between $10,000 to

$50,000. An abbreviated method of reporting is provided for a dormant controlled foreign corporation, but it is not clear if an unfunded foreign corporation is considered to be dormant.

A Form 926 is required by a U.S. transferor of property to a foreign corporation. Generally, this form is required for transfers of property in exchange for stock in the foreign corporation. The penalty for a failure to file the form is 10% of the fair market value of the property at the time of the transfer.

A Form 8621 is required by a U.S. shareholder of a Passive Foreign Investment Company (PFIC). However, it is not mandatory to file this form unless there is (1) a distribution of income from a passive foreign investment company (PFIC) in which a U.S. person is a shareholder or (2) a disposition of the shares of a PFIC by sale, gift, death and most types of otherwise tax free exchanges or redemptions. Notwithstanding, U.S. shareholders of a PFIC may choose to file this form on an annual basis to report income. If the income of the fund is not reported on an annual basis, there is a very punitive method of taxation of distributions of fund income or dispositions of fund shares.

A Form 8865 is required of U.S. persons with respect to certain controlled foreign partnerships. This form is required to be filed with the income tax return of each U.S. partner of a foreign partnership. In most respects it is a combination of the U.S. Form 1065 partnership return and the Form 5471 return for controlled foreign corporations. The penalties for failing to file the form or for failing to file it on a timely basis are the same as for foreign corporations, which is $10,000 per year for a failure to file and the loss of 10% of available foreign tax credits for filing late.

A Form 8832 is required for an election to be taxed as a disregarded entity. There is no penalty for not filing this form, but filing it on a timely basis can alleviate many of the tax problems that are caused because of being a shareholder, officer or director of a foreign corporation. A foreign limited liability company and foreign corporation will be treated as a foreign corporation for U.S. tax purposes unless the owners make an election to be treated as a partnership (two or more owners) or as a disregarded entity (one owner). Making the election by filing this form is optional, but if the form is not filed within 75 days after the formation of the entity, the default treatment will be to treat it as a foreign corporation.

A Form 8858 Information Return of U.S. persons with respect to foreign disregarded entities is required so that the IRS has assurance U.S. persons with foreign disregarded entities are reporting the income from those entities. It is to be filed with the income tax return of the U.S. person or corporation that is a shareholder or partner of a foreign entity that is treated as a disregarded entity. A $10,000 penalty is imposed for each year of each controlled foreign corporation or controlled foreign partnership for a failure to file this form within the time prescribed.

As noted elsewhere, a critical, too often overlooked, reporting requirement is Form TDF 90-22.1. This is the report of foreign bank and financial accounts discussed earlier. U.S. persons who have direct or indirect authority over, or a financial interest in, a foreign financial account may be required to report certain information about each account on or before June 30th of the year following the preceding calendar year, if the aggregate value of all foreign financial accounts is greater than $10,000 at any time during the preceding calendar year. A willful failure to file the form is subject to severe civil and criminal penalties, which includes civil and criminal penalties of up to $500,000, and imprisonment of up to five years. Congress has recently introduced a smaller penalty of up to $10,000 for a non-willful failure to file the form, effective for filing dates after October 22, 2004. Keep in mind this is simply as a result of a U.S. citizen failing to report signing power over assets in an offshore bank account, and includes failure to file a report, supply information, or for filing a false or fraudulent report.

The above penalties can *sometimes* be waived or reduced at the discretion of the IRS if the taxpayer can show a 'reasonable cause' for a failure to file or for a failure to file by the due date of the form or return. Reasonable cause might include such things as:

- A mistake made despite ordinary business care and prudence
- Forgetfulness
- Ignorance of the law
- Death, serious illness or unavoidable absence
- Inability to obtain records

- Inability to obtain tax forms
- Return was filed at the wrong IRS office
- Followed advice from a tax adviser
- Followed oral advice from the IRS
- IRS error

These are reasonable cause areas as defined by the IRS, not automatic waivers out of a tax penalty. The best bet is simply to make sure you, or someone you trust, is properly and timely filing necessary forms.

Is "ignorance of the law" an argument in tax disputes? Considering the horrendous volumes of text on tax code requirements, one would think this is reasonable. However, I wouldn't bet the ranch on it.

Now that you understand you have income tax and tax reporting requirements as an international investor, let's look at some of the remaining legal ways for U.S. citizens to save taxes while living or investing offshore.

CHAPTER TWENTY THREE

Legal Ways to Save Taxes Offshore

If you are a U.S. citizen or tax resident, by now you are probably completely gun shy against investing anywhere beyond your back yard. However, now its time to bring you back into the light and let you know there are still viable, legal ways to save taxes when investing offshore.

Many thanks to Vern Jacobs and the Offshore Press in their contributions identifying legal ways to save taxes offshore, the many tax reporting requirements, and other tax issues throughout this book. Recently he and Richard Duke published the book "Legal Ways to Save Taxes Offshore & Onshore." According to Vern, there seems to be a continuing interest by U.S. taxpayers in using offshore trusts, offshore investments and foreign corporations (or international business companies) to save taxes.

Unfortunately, there are many dodgy promoters – and just plain crooks – who are eager to take your money by selling you a packaged product allegedly to save you taxes or solve asset protection issues. While there are excellent offshore and international planning structures available from a small number of qualified professionals in this arena, with few exceptions, many offshore *prepackaged* trusts and other structures won't stand up to a serious inquiry by the IRS.

To summarize, a U.S. citizen or tax resident basically has four choices regarding taxes:

(1) He can engage in tax evasion with some kind of offshore arrangement and spend the rest of his life looking over his shoulder for the long arm of the IRS,

(2) He can just pay the taxes that the U.S. requires and complain about it,

(3) He can take advantage of every opportunity that is permitted by the tax law – but without engaging in a felony that could result in spending some time in jail, or

(4) He can relinquish his citizenship and residence on a permanent basis. Future income earned outside the U.S. will not be subject

to U.S. taxes, but certain types of U.S. source income may be taxable.

The U.S. seeks to tax the worldwide income of its citizens and tax residents – subject to only a very few exceptions – which are discussed below. However, this same principle means that any legal method of tax deferral or minimization within the U.S. is available anywhere in the world, unless of course there is an exception in the law regarding the use of various tax benefits outside the U.S.

To a very large extent, the international section of the U.S. tax law is a set of extensive exceptions to the various tax rules that apply within the U.S. Reports are available from Offshore Press describing legal ways that are available to save or defer taxes either in the U.S. or outside the U.S. The following information is a brief review of the various tax avoidance methods that are currently legal (if implemented correctly) and are only available to taxpayers outside the U.S. Because they are sanctioned by the tax code, they are far safer from attack by the IRS than the methods that are not sanctioned by some part of the tax law.

The Foreign Earned Income Exclusion (Section 911):

Up to $82,400 per year of income earned outside the U.S. while living and working outside the U.S. is exempt from U.S. income tax. If the employer is a foreign person, there is no RCA tax or Medicaid tax, although there may be a similar tax in the foreign country. If a married couple works and lives outside the U.S., they can each earn as much as $82,400 per year that is free of U.S. income, FICA and Medicaid taxes. This exempt amount will be indexed for inflation in future years. The U.S. citizen or resident must live outside the U.S. for at least 330 days in any 12 consecutive months. Take note: Congress has been "tweaking" this area of law even against loud objections from big corporations with large numbers of overseas employees as noted earlier.

Controlled Foreign Corporation ("CFC") with Only Business Income:

A U.S. person or company may own 100% of the stock of a foreign corporation and not be required to pay any U.S. income taxes on any profits of that foreign corporation. The short explanation is that the foreign corporation must be engaged in a trade or business in the country where it is based and must not have any passive investment income or any income from dealing on favorable terms with any U.S. shareholders or related persons. There are very strict and onerous rules in dealing with a CFC.

Non-Controlled Foreign Business Corporations:

The onerous rules that apply to U.S. shareholders of controlled foreign corporations can be avoided if no combination of five or fewer unrelated U.S. persons own more than 50% of the company. However, non-resident alien family members or unrelated foreign entities are not counted as U.S. shareholders. The discussion about the CFC tax rules deals with the traps that lie in wait for the taxpayer who does not get qualified help in organizing a foreign corporation and those same rules make it nearly impossible to avoid the CFC rules with the use of a foreign trust, bearer shares, nominee owners and similar schemes. But so long as the corporation ownership is either dispersed or so long as half the stock of the corporation is owned by foreign individuals, then a foreign corporation that is engaged in a trade or business could result in significant tax deferral.

An important qualification regarding CFCs is that the income must be from a trade or business that is not being managed from within the U.S. by means of an Internet connection to a web site on a foreign web server.

Non-Grantor Foreign Trust for Beneficiaries:

Foreign trusts (for purposes of U.S. tax law) are no longer useful as a way to defer taxes for U.S. beneficiaries of a foreign trust funded by U.S. citizens or residents during the lifetime of the persons who provide the funding. However, a foreign trust can become a non-grantor trust after the death of the founder/grantor. Income earned after the death of the U.S. grantors will not be subject to U.S. income tax until the income is distributed to the beneficiaries. Income that is not distributed can be accumulated and re-invested free of U.S. income and estate taxes for multiple generations. (This may create an opportunity for some settlors to initially create a U.S. Domestic Grantor trust, and then at their death allow the trust to become a foreign trust for tax purposes.)

U.S. Virgin Islands Residency:

The U.S. Virgin Islands offer very enticing tax benefits for immigrants who come with money. They seek retirees with Social Security or pension benefits, business entrepreneurs who will create a business to create jobs in the USVI and investors who will invest in USVI businesses. But there is a small catch.

This tax break only applies to bone fide residents of the USVI. Some U.S. taxpayers have attempted to circumvent the rules by establishing a USVI residence on paper but who continued to live and work in the U.S.

Expatriation and Inversions:

Over the centuries, taxpayers who felt they were overburdened by taxes often voted with their feet. They left their home country to pursue opportunity in countries with less government and therefore with fewer taxes.

Although the individual income tax in the U.S. is not more than most industrial countries, the combination of the income tax, the Social Security tax, the Medicaid tax, state income taxes, property taxes, sales taxes, the inflation tax and ultimately the estate tax creates the most burdensome tax regime in the world for the more affluent members of the U.S. Few lower income taxpayers pay any significant income taxes and would not be subject to any federal estate tax.

As noted earlier, there is a disproportionate amount of taxes paid by the top 50% of wage earners. While lower income citizens are far more likely to expatriate for employment opportunities or for family reasons, high-income citizens may be motivated to leave because of taxes. Individual expatriation is covered in more detail in the following chapters.

A corporation can also go through the process of expatriating, referred to as an "inversion." A U.S. based company with operations in multiple countries may discover that it is paying a very high tax on the income the corporation is earning in subsidiary corporations based in low tax countries. Moving the base of a multi-national corporation to a tax haven does not reduce any U.S. tax on the business within the U.S., but it does help to reduce or eliminate U.S. taxes on operations in low tax countries.

The U.S. government has made a number of efforts to curtail this practice for the reason of not wanting to lose the tax revenue. Often, uninformed politicians wrap themselves in the flag and denounce the companies that expatriate, but they won't reform the complex international tax laws that make it difficult for U.S. corporations to compete in the international market place.

There you have it... what's presently left for U.S. citizens and tax residents for offshore tax benefits is small by comparison to what it once was. Considering that most other citizens of the world don't carry such a heavy burden, it is amazing how the U.S. government continues to dish out such severe punishment for those it claims it serves. I will leave it to you to decide if Americans are delusional about their apparent #1 standing in the world (the Epilogue dismisses some of these myths).

Just one more word about what the taxing situation looks like for the future (so hang in there) before exploring the ultimate tax plan – denouncing U.S. citizenship.

CHAPTER TWENTY FOUR

A Taxing Global Future

If the past sheds light on the future, which is usually does, then what does the future for taxation hold?

As you have repeatedly seen, the U.S. tax system imposes a draconian tax on the worldwide income of any U.S. citizen, permanent resident or any entity formed in the U.S. The U.S. system also taxes the U.S. owners of any foreign entities such as foreign trusts, foreign corporations and various foreign investments.

Notwithstanding foreign income tax credits, there are numerous restrictions and limitations, and they are constantly undergoing changes in Congress. For example, a U.S. corporation can claim a credit for foreign taxes paid by a foreign subsidiary, but not if the foreign corporation is owned by an individual or a partnership. Another example is that if a value added tax is imposed on the profits earned in a foreign country, the VAT is not allowed as a credit against the U.S. taxes on the same income because the VAT is not deemed to be an income tax..... Got it?

And for those familiar with the dreaded AMT (alternative minimum tax), can you say: *"watch foreign tax credits disappear when AMT is applied"?* I knew you could.

As noted previously, there are many good reasons for an international trust to be classified as a U.S. domestic grantor trust for tax purposes vs. a foreign trust. One of the strongest arguments for the US grantor trust is the heavy penalties for failure to file timely forms for a foreign trust, which can cost the taxpayer 35% of the assets in the trust. For clients, I personally recommend the U.S. domestic grantor trust for integrated international asset protection planning, offshore investing and pre-migration planning, since this variety of international trust is far more "user" friendly.

Regrettably, many politicians seem to think that the answer to every alleged social and political problem is imposing higher taxes. Now, even the United Nations wants to create an International Tax Organization (ITO) that would have the power to interfere with national tax policies.

This crazy idea first surfaced two years ago in a report from the world body's "High-Level Panel on Financing for Development." Since then, the U.N. has been working to turn it into reality. Former-U.N. General Secretary Kofi Annan recently called for the creation of a global tax commission. But no matter what it's called, an international bureaucracy with power over tax policy would be an assault on individual sovereignty, wherever located.

An international tax organization, of course, would mean higher taxes and bigger government…. and more headaches for you and me. Indeed, U.N. officials have been quite open about their intentions. The chairman of the U.N. panel that first endorsed the creation of an ITO said that it would "take a lead role in restraining tax competition." According to the misguided U.N. mentality, it's unfair for one country to have lower taxes than another. These narrow-minded bureaucrats simply don't understand that money goes where it is treated best, as people migrate to countries where better opportunities exist.

And guess what? The U.N. also wants the power to levy its own taxes. The original report looked at two options, a tax on currency transactions and a tax on energy consumption. This is only the tip of the iceberg as the U.N. has endorsed taxation of the Internet, particularly a tax on e-mail.

But the award winning worst U.N. idea belongs to a proposal to give governments permanent taxing rights over emigrants. The U.N. thinks it is "unfair" when talented people leave high-tax socialist nations and move to freer countries offering better opportunities. The bureaucrats are proposing to let governments tax expatriates' income earned in other nations.

While you might chuckle at the above proposals, the reality is that a good bureaucrat has never seen a tax he or she didn't like.

Another reason we should worry is that the U.N. is just one of several international bureaucracies working to undermine fiscal sovereignty. The Paris-based Organization for Economic Cooperation and Development (OECD) targets "harmful tax competition" and the Brussels-based European Union enthusiastically backs "tax harmonization."

Clearly we have to stand up for our rights – unless we want to see our tax bills soar and our quality of life suffer. From an unknown author, we conclude this section on tax compliance with the following:

Taxes

Tax his land,
Tax his bed,
Tax the table
At which he's fed.

Tax his tractor,
Tax his mule,
Teach him taxes
are the rule.

Tax his cow,
Tax his goat,
Tax his pants,
Tax his coat.

Tax his ties,
Tax his shirt,
Tax his work,
Tax his dirt.

Tax his tobacco,
Tax his drink,
Tax him if he
Tries to think.

Tax his chips,
Tax his beers,
If he cries, then
Tax his tears.

Tax his car,
Tax his gas,
Find other ways
To tax his ass.

Tax all he has
then let him know,
that you won't be done
till he has no dough.

When he screams & hollers,
Then tax him some more,
Tax him till
he's good and sore.

Then tax his coffin,
Tax his grave,
Tax the sod in
Which he's laid.

Put these words
upon his tomb,
"Taxes drove me
to my doom..."

When he's gone,
Do not relax,
Its time to apply
The inheritance tax.

Think for a moment how many of the following taxes you pay every year, either directly or indirectly:

Accounts Receivable Tax, Alternative Minimum Tax (AMT), Building Permit Tax, CDL license Tax, Cigarette Tax, Corporate Income Tax, Dog License Tax, Federal Income Tax, Federal Unemployment Tax (FUTA), Fishing License Tax, Food License Tax, Fuel permit tax, Gasoline Tax, Goods and Service Tax (GST) Hunting License Tax, Inheritance Tax, Interest expense, Inventory tax, IRS Interest Charges, IRS Penalties (tax on top of tax), Liquor Tax, Luxury Taxes, Marriage License Tax, Medicare Tax, Property Tax, Real Estate Tax, Service charge taxes, Social Security Tax, Road usage taxes, Sales Tax, Recreational Vehicle Tax, School Tax, State Income Tax, State Unemployment Tax (SUTA), Telephone federal excise tax, Telephone federal universal service fee tax, Telephone federal, state and local surcharge taxes, Telephone minimum usage surcharge tax, Telephone recurring and non-recurring charges tax, Telephone state and local tax, Telephone usage charge tax, Utility Taxes, Vehicle License Registration Tax, Vehicle Sales Tax, Watercraft registration Tax, Well Permit Tax, Workers Compensation Tax…. and how many other taxes did I fail to mention?

Not one of these taxes existed 100 years ago and the United States and most other major nations were on the edge of prospering in the world – and they had no national debt – with large middle classes, and Mom stayed home to raise the kids.

What happened to our brave new world? What can we do?

THE ULTIMATE TAX PLAN: DENOUNCING U.S. CITIZENSHIP

Just because a message reaches farther doesn't mean it is better.
Anonymous

CHAPTER TWENTY FIVE

Is the Ultimate Tax Plan Right for You?

If you are a U.S. citizen or tax resident looking for the ultimate and final step to remove U.S. tax burdens off of your shoulders, forever, then this might be for you! Admittedly, it is not for everyone!

As you know only too well, taxes take a major bite out of your income and your assets. As you saw earlier, not so surprising, is that the top income earners pay the majority of all taxes. Seems rather unfair, don't you think?

With tax loopholes mostly long gone from the earlier versions of the forever-changing tax codes, there is generally little you can do to shelter your income once your assets are income-producing. However, if you are willing to make a significant change in your citizenship, and perhaps are ready to move to that perfect island paradise you have always dreamed about, then there is one last option available to you to help protect and preserve your assets from ravenous tax burdens.

For some Americans, the American dream is being realized abroad. These adventurous individuals have pooled their money and taken their skills to over 100 different countries around the world. According to the U.S. State Department, more than 3.8 million Americans live abroad every year.

An estimated 200,000 to 250,000 Americans move out of the U.S. each and every year, but most of them are not true tax exiles. The vast majority of the individuals retain their U.S. citizenship. Many of them qualify for tax-free income under IRC 911 as discussed earlier.

The U.S. is facing a brain drain: 60 percent of Americans state that the U.S. quality of life is degenerating and they consider moving elsewhere for a better quality of life; expatriates include some of America's wealthiest and most educated native-born citizens; approximately 25% of college educated and 25% of income earners above $50,000 per year have considered leaving the U.S.; and more skilled workers are leaving the U.S. than are entering. Increasingly these individuals are searching for the American dream elsewhere.

The option of expatriation is the final step for some U.S. citizens who are fed up with U.S. taxes, discouraged by litigation-gone-wild, severe limitations on privacy, and over zealous political agendas. These individuals are willing to leave America. The only way that a U.S. citizen can legally eliminate all U.S. income tax and estate taxes is by completely eliminating all connections to its tax consuming Uncle Sam. In other words, you must completely expatriate yourself altogether from the U.S. including giving up citizenship.

Those that have gone the final distance include businessman John Templeton, of Templeton Funds, when he moved to the Bahamas and saved more than $100,000,000 in taxes in his well-known investment fund.

Other well-known individuals include Campbell Soup heir John "Ippy" Dorrance III moving to Ireland; and Michael Dingman, chairman of Abex and a Ford Motor Company director moving to the Bahamas; Kenneth Dart, heir to the billion-dollar Dart Container fortune moving to the Bahamas; Ted Arison, head of Carnival Cruise Line moving to Israel; and the head of Locktite Corporation, Fred Kreible, moving to the Turks and Caicos.

The list goes on. Why do they do it? The reasons are vast and many, but sometimes these individuals are motivated by the unfair and burdensome U.S. income and estate tax laws.

Becoming an expatriate means moving abroad so that you are no longer a U.S. resident for federal income tax purposes. This also means that you will need to change your domicile to a suitable foreign country so that you are no longer a U.S. domiciliary for tax purposes. And finally, you will need to give up your U.S. citizenship so that you are not subject to income taxes on your worldwide income or estate taxes.

Other factors to consider will include making certain that your status is not tainted by the status of your spouse. In other words, your spouse should take the same steps as you to make sure that your jointly owned property is removed from the jurisdiction of the U.S. You will then want to make sure that all of your income is derived from foreign sources and that your property is owned in countries other than the U.S.

Importantly, you will need to consider the timing of making these property transfers, and consider how it will affect your status as an expatriate. You will need to give consideration as to the beneficiaries of your estate and the tax impact on them if they do not become tax exiles. So how do you go about giving up your U.S. citizenship?

First, you need to acquire citizenship elsewhere. Then, if you don't plan on living in your newly adopted country of citizenship, you will need to find a country that is willing to accept you as a resident you and your family can call home. Some countries require a time period to obtain residency, others will require work permits, and in others, you can purchase residency for a set dollar amount or investment into the country.

The residency and citizenship rules vary from country to country and are in constant flux, and can take weeks to months – and even years – to complete. What looks good today, disappears tomorrow. And when thinking about residency for purposes of citizenship, remember that all passports are not equal when it comes to traveling to other countries. Some countries will allow visa free travel, and others will not. If you wish to return to the U.S., some passports will be more easily accepted than others.

When you abandon your U.S. citizenship, you are required to make an official denouncement, generally through the U.S. Consulates Office by declaring your intentions.

And beware: Uncle Sam will try one last time to get into your wallet before you leave.

Whatever you choose, be aware of your options. Only when you are educated about the alternatives and make a voluntary choice based upon the options, can you be said to be living life by choice. Maybe that choice is at home, or maybe that choice is offshore on your island paradise. Maybe it's a combination of both.

Next we look closer at the important details for those considering renouncing citizenship.

CHAPTER TWENTY SIX

Expatriation: Giving Up Your USA Citizenship

So you have (almost) decided to give up U.S. citizenship.

The U.S. is the only major country in the world that imposes income taxes and estate taxes on its citizens or long term residents (U.S. 'persons') no matter where they live, where their assets are located or where their income is realized. A U.S. person could spend a lifetime in a foreign country and still be subject to the U.S. tax laws…. draconian at its worst.

By contrast, most other countries only impose income taxes on the income of their residents. Canada, for example, imposes tax on the worldwide income only on their residents. Likewise for New Zealand and Australia and U.K. and most of the rest of the world. But if other citizens move to a low tax country, they generally have no legal duty to pay taxes to their departed homeland after moving. Similar rules apply in most countries. Thus, tax havens are valid and legal for nearly everyone in the world, except for U.S. persons. The only way a U.S. person can escape from the yoke of U.S. taxes is to give up his or her citizenship and residency.

There are huge tax advantages to expatriate for U.S. citizens and tax residents who have substantial investment assets that can be moved to a low tax country. By changing citizenship to a foreign country, the U.S. person will naturally be subject to local taxes on any salaries or business profits in that country, but can avoid U.S. taxes on that income. The expatriate may also avoid taxes entirely on the income derived from any assets kept outside the newly adopted country. And, expatriation can be an effective way to avoid huge estate taxes on large estates.

When expatriating, the U.S. imposes income taxes on unrealized gains derived by U.S. citizens or long term residents for up to ten years after they give up their citizenship. U.S. estate taxes would also be imposed on any U.S. based assets for up to ten years after expatriation. However, any future earned income and any investment income realized from new savings outside the U.S. could be arranged to be free of U.S. taxes.

And too, any "after tax" assets moved outside the U.S. could be free of U.S. estate taxes. "After tax" assets are those assets with no deferred income or unrealized gains. Basically, the current expatriation tax scheme seeks to collect the income taxes on all untaxed income or gains at the time of expatriation. The above is an extremely simplified explanation of some very elaborate and complicated tax rules and good tax counsel on these issues is essential.

By way of example, consider how a U.S. person might obtain Canadian citizenship and thereafter expatriate from the U.S.

Before you expatriate from the U.S. you must first acquire citizenship through full time residence in Canada. A Canadian passport is respected throughout the world. The entire process takes approximately five years once living in Canada. In the interim, you will need to have a job or enough assets while living in Canada. During the five years, you will continue to be subject to U.S. taxes on all of your income. If you are required to pay taxes to Canada on your income, you can deduct the Canadian taxes from the taxes you owe to the U.S.

After you have acquired Canadian citizenship and your new passport, you can then renounce your U.S. citizenship. Based upon current laws, if you have less than $2 million in net assets you would not be subject to any U.S. taxes on any future income from foreign sources.

Thereafter, you could then move to a low or zero tax country. There are a variety of small countries that offer generous tax subsidies to retired persons, investors and business entrepreneurs. You can then become free of any tax obligations to Canada, if you follow the proper procedures for a permanent change in residence.

If your net worth at the time is less than $2 million, you would also be free of any future U.S. taxes except on U.S. source income.

On the other hand, if you have a net worth of more than $2 million, you will be subject to U.S. taxes for up to ten years after expatriating on certain types of U.S. source income.... generally meaning deferred income assets. However, you will not be subject to any foreign source income after you expatriate.

The above example is but one of numerous methods to leave the U.S. tax system behind. And if you plan properly, you could – theoretically –

completely remove yourself from all taxing jurisdictions, worldwide, and live income tax free. Other countries offer shorter time periods in which to acquire citizenship, and "economic" citizenship is also an instant option to speed up the process.

The bottom line is that you need to plan ahead to expatriate if you are not already a dual citizen. And too, this area of law has recently become under closer scrutiny as more U.S. individuals look to call home elsewhere.

A 1996 immigration law included a provision that basically made it either impossible or extremely difficult for a U.S. citizen who expatriates in order to save taxes to return to the U.S. to visit. That forces a family to leave relatives behind or to move an entire family simultaneously. Even though not apparently enforced, it is unsure how much this law has deterred expatriation.

The *Health Insurance Portability Act of 1996* revised expatriating rules so that any citizen or permanent resident with a net worth of $500,000 or more, or with an average tax bill for the previous three years of more than $100,000, would be presumed to have a tax motivated reason for expatriation.

In late 2002, several members of Congress proposed an "exit tax" on anyone who expatriates, but this proposal was defeated. It has been re-introduced (and defeated) each year since 2002 and is likely to be included in future tax bills.

Of most recent, in 2004 substantial changes were introduced by the *American Jobs Creation Act of 2004* – mostly for the benefit of U.S. citizens or residents who want to expatriate. For individuals who expatriate after June 3, 2005, the net worth test has been increased to $2 million and the test for the average tax bill (previous three years) was increased to $124,000 for the year of 2004. Both amounts are to be indexed for inflation.

And as I type this today, Congress is on the verge of considering another outrageous new law that would impose the first-ever "exit tax" on U.S. expatriate citizens and residents. In this case, the bones are buried in the "Small Business and Work Opportunity Act."

Right now, this bill is stuck in a conference committee in Congress.

If it passes, it could include a little-known provision, which demands that expatriates pay a tax on all unrealized gains of their worldwide estate. The gains will be assessed based on the fair market value of the expatriate's assets and the tax due within 90 days of expatriation.

This exit tax applies to assets held in retirement plans and trusts, both domestic and foreign. The only thing it doesn't apply to is U.S. real estate investments, which remain subject to U.S. tax under existing law.

As presently set out in the bill before Congress, gains would be taxed as ordinary income as high as 35%, or capital gains at the 15% or 25% rate. When the assets are actually sold, no further U.S. tax will be due; however the gain might be taxed again by the country in which you reside, leading to double taxation on the same income.

How this new law would apply to retirement plans is particularly unfair. These gains would be taxed at the expatriate's top marginal tax rate – up to 35% – and would not generally be eligible for the lower 15% long-term capital gains rate.

And expatriates who must withdraw assets from their retirement plan to pay the tax under age 59-1/2, will be hit with a 10% penalty tax on top of the exit tax. What's worse, when distributions are actually made, the country where the expatriate resides could tax those distributions again.

Under the pending bill the first U.S. $600,000 of gains will be excluded from the exit tax. A married couple could exclude U.S. $1.2 million if both were expatriating. The exclusion will increase each year as the cost of living adjusts.

Since the publication of an article in *Forbes* magazine in 1994 describing a handful of wealthy Americans who had given up their U.S. citizenship to escape taxes, the image of former wealthy citizens fleeing the homeland to live tax-free in tropical paradise has been an irresistible ongoing media headline. There wouldn't even be a story to tell if U.S. citizens, unlike citizens of the rest of the world, were taxed on their residence and not over-taxed on the basis of their citizenship.

Even in high tax countries like the United Kingdom, Japan, Canada, Australia, and elsewhere, citizens need only to leave those countries and become non-resident for an extended period to stop paying taxes in their home country. But not the United States: it taxes all the earnings of all its citizens, regardless where they reside, and for how long they live outside the U.S., forever.

Given the extreme attitudes of patriotism flocking the halls of Congress, it is not surprising that the political know-it-alls wrapped in the American flag would enact an exit tax on so called "rich" expatriates. But the exit tax goes further, since the tax burden would also affect hundreds of thousands of wealthy long-term green card holders who are not U.S. citizens, and no longer reside in the U.S.

Needless to say, if this bill becomes law, it will also discourage successful foreigners from taking up residence in the U.S. so they don't get caught up in the exit tax trap. As the U.S. continues in its downward spiral with its lack of global competitiveness, this only serves to strike another nail in the coffin of doom.

And beware, there is also a harsh penalty for those who might be tempted not to comply with the law: anyone who does not comply with the new U.S. Tax Code will be denied entry to the United States.

By enacting the outlandish exit tax, the United States would firmly join the ranks of Nazi Germany, the former Soviet Union and South Africa, all of which confiscated the assets of wealthy emigrants and imposed currency restrictions.

Admittedly, the exit tax is estimated to raise only a small amount of taxes. But the estimates do not include the loss revenues from investors and highly talented individuals who would decline to establish U.S. residence or citizenship to avoid such harsh tax treatment.

Is the exit tax unconstitutional? Probably, but this doesn't seem to matter to Congress.

The Declaration of Independence cites the right to expatriate as a fundamental "law of nature." And the U.S. Constitution guarantees the right to end U.S. citizenship, to live and travel abroad freely, and to acquire citizenship from other nations. All of these rights have been affirmed by the U.S. Supreme Court as noted elsewhere in the book.

The tax impact regarding expatriation is under constant scrutiny and is in a state of flux. Particularly with the Democrat controlled Congress, we are sure to see more debate on the expat-tax related issues and changes for the worse for those with thoughts of expatriating.

The bottom line: preplanning is an essential part of expatriating if you are a high-net worth or high-income individual, even if not expatriating for tax motivated reasons.

As a U.S. citizen or tax resident, there is one other area of concern: how to maintain federal retirement benefits, known as Social Security?

DON'T LEAVE YOUR SOCIAL SECURITY BENEFITS BEHIND

"Eighty percent of success is showing up."
Woody Allen

CHAPTER TWENTY SEVEN

Social Security Benefits & You

Last but not least, many citizens worldwide have contributed into government sponsored forced savings and retirement programs. U.S. citizens and foreign wage earners within the U.S. were led to believe the purpose of Social Security was to provide for a security net for old age. For years I can remember it being called a "forced savings" plan: It was my money in the system, and always to be there when I needed it most. Right Dorothy, click your heels twice!

Week after week, month after month, year after year, and dollar after dollar you were forced to contribute into this social savings plan, which was supposedly your security net. After all, if it wasn't your money, then whose was it? We earned the money, paid taxes on it, and it was withheld (supposedly) for us until retirement.

Silly us.... taken in by one of the greatest frauds of all time.

Not only are there huge social security deficits, but the prospects of increasing larger shortfalls for the large number of baby boomers in the years ahead looks bleaker each day. To make matters worse, depending on where you live you might not even have a "right" to receive *your* money back from your forced savings account.

Planning ahead for your choice of a retirement destination outside of the U.S. can make a significant difference in how much, if any at all, you receive of your Social Security benefits.

Your Social Security payments may vary widely if you are living outside of the United States.

First, what does "Outside of the USA" mean to the Social Security Administration? This means you are not in one of the 50 states, the District of Columbia, Puerto Rico, the U.S. Virgin Islands, Guam, the Northern Mariana Islands or American Samoa. Once you have been out of the U.S. for at least 30 days in a row, you are considered to be outside the country until you return and stay in the U.S. for at least 30 days in a row. If you are not a U.S. citizen, you also may have to prove that you were lawfully present in the U.S. for that 30-day period.

What happens to your Social Security payments when you are outside of the USA? *The simple rule is that if you are a U.S. citizen, you may receive your Social Security payments outside the U.S. as long as you are eligible for them.* However, there are certain countries to which payments will not be sent.

Presently, if you are a citizen of one of the following countries, Social Security payments will keep coming no matter how long you stay outside the U.S., as long as you are eligible for the payments: Austria, Belgium, Canada, Chile, Finland, France, Germany, Greece, Ireland, Israel, Italy, Japan, Korea (South), Luxembourg, Netherlands, Norway, Portugal, Spain, Sweden, Switzerland, and the United Kingdom.

If you are a citizen of one of the countries listed below, you also may receive your payments as long as you are outside the U.S., unless you are receiving your payments as a dependent or survivor. In that case, there are additional requirements you have to meet: Albania, Antigua and Barbuda, Argentina, Bahamas, Barbados, Belize, Bolivia, Bosnia-Herzegovina, Brazil, Burkina Faso, Colombia, Costa Rica, Côte d'Ivoire, Croatia, Cyprus, Czech Republic, Denmark, Dominica, Dominican Republic, Ecuador, El Salvador, Gabon, Grenada, Guatemala, Guyana, Hungary, Iceland, Jamaica, Jordan, Latvia, Liechtenstein, Lithuania, Macedonia, Malta, Marshall Islands, Mexico, Micronesia, Monaco, Nicaragua, Palau, Panama, Peru, Philippines, Poland, St. Kitts and Nevis, St. Lucia, Samoa (formerly Western Samoa), San Marino, Serbia and Montenegro, Slovakia, Slovenia, Trinidad-Tobago, Turkey, Uruguay, and Venezuela.

If you are not a U.S. citizen or a citizen of one of the other countries listed, your payments will stop after you have been outside the U.S. for six full calendar months unless you meet one of the following exceptions:

- You were eligible for monthly Social Security benefits before December 1956; or

- You are in the active military or naval service of the U.S.; or

- The worker on whose record your benefits are based had railroad work which was treated as covered employment by the Social Security program; or

- The worker on whose record your benefits are based died while in the U.S. military service or as a result of a service-connected disability and was not dishonorably discharged; or

- You are a *resident* of a country with which the U.S. has a Social Security agreement. Currently, these countries are:

    Australia, Austria, Belgium, Canada, Chile, Finland, France, Germany, Greece, Ireland, Italy, Japan, Korea (South), Luxembourg, Netherlands, Norway, Portugal, Spain, Sweden, Switzerland, and the United Kingdom.

However, the agreements with Austria, Belgium, Germany, Sweden and Switzerland permit you to receive benefits as a dependent or survivor of a worker while you reside in the foreign country only if the worker is a U.S. citizen or a citizen of your country of residence; or you are a citizen of one of the countries listed below, and the worker on whose record your benefits are based lived in the U.S. for at least 10 years or earned at least 40 credits under the U.S. Social Security system (if you are receiving benefits as a dependent or survivor, see additional requirements): Afghanistan, Australia, Bangladesh, Bhutan, Botswana, Burma, Burundi, Cameroon, Cape Verde, Central African Rep. Chad, China, Congo, Rep. of Ethiopia, Fiji, Gambia, Ghana, St. Vincent & Grenadines, Senegal, Sierra Leone, Singapore, Solomon Islands, Somalia, South Africa, Sri Lanka, Sudan, Swaziland, Taiwan, Tanzania, Thailand, Togo, Tonga, Tunisia, Uganda and Yemen.

Note that if you are not a citizen of one of the countries listed above, you cannot use this exception.

If you are not a U.S. citizen and none of these exceptions apply to you, your payments will stop after you have been outside the U.S. for six full months. Once this happens, your payments cannot be started again until you come back and stay in the U.S. for a whole calendar month. You have to be in the U.S. on the first minute of the first day of a month and stay through the last minute of the last day of that month. In addition, you may be required to prove that you have been lawfully present in the U.S. for the full calendar month.

And there are also additional residency requirements for dependents and survivors. If you receive benefits as a dependent or survivor of the worker, special requirements may affect your right to receive Social

Security payments while you are outside the U.S. If you are not a U.S. citizen, you must have lived in the U.S. for at least five years. During that five years, the family relationship on which benefits are based must have existed.

Children may meet this residency requirement on their own or may be considered to meet the residency requirement if it is met by the worker and other parent (if any). However, children adopted outside the U.S. will not be paid outside the U.S., even if the residency requirement is met.

The residency requirement will not apply to you if you meet any of the following conditions:

- You were initially eligible for monthly benefits before January 1, 1985; or

- You are entitled on the record of a worker who died while in the U.S. military service or as a result of a service-connected disease or injury; or

- You are a citizen of one of the following countries: Austria, Belgium, Canada, Chile, Finland, France, Germany, Greece, Ireland, Israel, Italy, Japan, Korea (South), Luxembourg, Netherlands, Norway, Portugal, Spain, Sweden, Switzerland, or the United Kingdom.

- You are a resident of one of the countries with which the U.S. has a Social Security agreement. These countries are listed below: Australia, Austria, Belgium, Canada, Chile, Finland, France, Germany, Greece, Ireland, Italy, Japan, Korea (South), Luxembourg, Netherlands, Norway, Portugal, Spain, Sweden, Switzerland, or the United Kingdom.

And there are certain countries the USA will not send social security benefits. U.S. Treasury Department regulations prohibit sending payments to you if you are in Cuba or North Korea. If you are a U.S. citizen and are in Cuba or North Korea, you can receive all of your payments that were withheld once you leave that country and go to another country where they will send payments. Generally, if you are not a U.S. citizen, you cannot receive any payments for months in which you live in one of these countries, even though you leave that country and satisfy all other requirements.

Furthermore, Social Security restrictions prohibit sending payments to individuals in Cambodia, Vietnam or areas that were in the former Soviet Union (other than Armenia, Estonia, Latvia, Lithuania and Russia). Generally, you cannot receive payments while you are in one of these countries, and they will not send your payments to anyone for you. However, exceptions can be made for certain eligible beneficiaries in countries other than Cuba or North Korea.

If you do not qualify for payment you can move from one of these countries to another country where they will send payments and you can receive all the benefits for which you were eligible except when you were in one of the listed countries.

Now you have the skinny on Social Security benefits.

If you are not satisfied with the above simplification, *www.social security.gov* is a valuable resource for further information about Social Security's programs. If you are outside the United States, see the list of offices where you can get more information. If you are in the United States, you can call toll-free at 1-800-772-1213 from 7 a.m. to 7 p.m., Monday through Friday. All calls are *allegedly* treated confidentially.... at least so they say.

CHAPTER TWENTY EIGHT

Are Americans Delusional?

The western world offers a quality of living never experienced in history. But many Americans, while living in a land still offering great opportunities today, are awash in numbing propaganda believing the U.S. is the best and *only* option worth considering.

No concept lies more firmly embedded in the national character than the notion that the USA is "No. 1," "the greatest." The broadcast media are, in essence, continuous advertisements for the brand name "America is No. 1." Any office seeker saying otherwise would be committing political suicide. In fact, anyone saying otherwise would be labeled "un-American."

America is an "empire," isn't it? Sure it is. An empire without a manufacturing base. An empire that must borrow $2 billion a day from its competitors in order to function. Yet the delusion is ineradicable: America is No. 1.

For those Americans unwilling to accept or understand that there are global possibilities equal to or even superior to the American dream, I offer the following collection of statistics, some admitted slightly dated, but nonetheless just as significant and getting worse each year. Most truths are so naked that people feel sorry for them and cover them up, at least a little bit.

Consider for a moment, if you will:

* Of the 20 richest countries of the world, the children of the United States rank dead last for the worst quality of life ranking worldwide (the Economist, Feb 14 2007).

* The United States is 49th in the world in literacy (the New York Times, Dec. 12, 2004).

* The United States ranked 28th out of 40 countries in mathematical literacy (NYT, Dec. 12, 2004).

* Twenty percent of Americans think the sun orbits the earth. Seventeen percent believe the earth revolves around the sun once a day (*The Week*, Jan. 7, 2005).

* "The International Adult Literacy Survey found that Americans with less than nine years of education scored worse than virtually all of the other countries" (Jeremy Rifkin's superbly documented book *The European Dream: How Europe's Vision of the Future Is Quietly Eclipsing the American Dream,* p.78).

* American workers are so ignorant and lack so many basic skills that American businesses spend $30 billion a year on remedial training (NYT, Dec. 12, 2004). No wonder corporate America seeks workers elsewhere for less!

* "The European Union leads the U.S. in the number of science and engineering graduates; public research and development (R&D) expenditures; and new capital raised" (*The European Dream*, p.70).

* "Europe surpassed the United States in the mid-1990s as the largest producer of scientific literature" (*The European Dream*, p.70).

* Nevertheless, Congress cut funds to the National Science Foundation. The agency will issue 1,000 fewer research grants this year (NYT, Dec. 21, 2004).

* Foreign applications to U.S. grad schools declined 28 percent in recent years and continue to decline. Foreign student enrollment on all levels fell for the first time in three decades, but increased greatly in Europe and China. Last year Chinese grad-school graduates in the U.S. dropped 56 percent, Indians 51 percent, South Koreans 28 percent (NYT, Dec. 21, 2004). America is not the place to be anymore.

* The World Health Organization "ranked the countries of the world in terms of overall health performance, and the U.S. [was]...37th." In the fairness of health care, America was 54th. "The irony is that the United States spends more per capita for health care than any other nation in the world" (*The European Dream*, pp.79-80). Pay more, get lots, lots less.

* "The U.S. and South Africa are the only two developed countries in the world that do not provide health care for all their citizens" (*The European Dream*, p.80). Excuse me, but since when is South Africa a "developed" country? Anyway, that's the company America is keeping.

* The 2005 pending Highway Bill with a total price tag of $295 billion

has hundreds of unrelated items, such as a huge exit tax on any American who leaves, then ends citizenship; as much as a 50% capital gains tax on almost all property! Other Nations that imposed such onerous taxes were Nazi Germany and apartheid South Africa. (Indianapolis Star, May 23, 2005).

* Lack of health insurance coverage causes 18,000 unnecessary American deaths a year. (That's six times the number of people killed on 9/11.) (NYT, Jan. 12, 2005.)

* "U.S. childhood poverty now ranks 22nd, or second to last, among the developed nations. Only Mexico scores lower" (*The European Dream*, p.81). Been to Mexico lately? Does it look "developed" to you? Yet it's the only "developed" country to score lower in childhood poverty.

* Twelve million American families–more than 10 percent of all U.S. households–"continue to struggle, and not always successfully, to feed themselves." Families that "had members who actually went hungry at some point last year" numbered 3.9 million (NYT, Nov. 22, 2004).

* The latest official half-yearly figures found American's prison and jail population at 2,131,180, an increase of 2.3 percent over 2003. The United States has incarcerated 726 people per 100,000 of its population, 7 to 10 times as many as most other democracies. The rate for England is 142 per 100,000, for France 91 and for Japan 58. It costs around $22,000 to lock up one person for a year. The United States spends about $57 billion annually on its prison and jail system (CNN/ Washington Rueters April 25, 2005).

* The United States is 41st in the world in infant mortality. Cuba scores higher (NYT, Jan. 12, 2005).

* Women are 70 percent more likely to die in childbirth in America than in Europe (NYT, Jan. 12, 2005).

* The leading cause of death of pregnant women in this country is murder (CNN, Dec. 14, 2004).

* "Of the 20 most developed countries in the world, the U.S. was dead last in the growth rate of total compensation to its workforce in the 1980s.... In the 1990s, the U.S. average compensation growth rate

grew only slightly, at an annual rate of about 0.1 percent" (*The European Dream*, p.39). Yet Americans work longer hours per year than any other industrialized country, and get less vacation time.

* "Sixty-one of the 140 biggest companies on the Global Fortune 500 rankings are European, while only 50 are U.S. companies" (*The European Dream*, p.66). "In a recent survey of the world's 50 best companies, conducted by Global Finance, all but one were European" (*The European Dream*, p.69).

* "Fourteen of the 20 largest commercial banks in the world today are European.... In the chemical industry, the European company BASF is the world's leader, and three of the top six players are European. In engineering and construction, three of the top five companies are European.... The two others are Japanese. Not a single American engineering and construction company is included among the world's top nine competitors. In food and consumer products, Nestlé and Unilever, two European giants, rank first and second, respectively, in the world. In the food and drugstore retail trade, two European companies...are first and second, and European companies make up five of the top ten. Only four U.S. companies are on the list" (*The European Dream*, p.68).

* The United States has lost 1.3 million jobs to China in the last decade (CNN, Jan. 12, 2005).

* U.S. employers eliminated 1 million jobs in 2004 (*The Week*, Jan. 14, 2005).

* Three million six hundred thousand Americans ran out of unemployment insurance last year; 1.8 million–one in five–unemployed workers are jobless for more than six months (NYT, Jan. 9, 2005).

* Japan, China, Taiwan, and South Korea hold 40 percent of our government debt. (That's why we talk nice to them.) "By helping keep mortgage rates from rising, China played an enormous and little-noticed role in sustaining the American housing boom" (NYT, Dec. 4, 2004). Read that twice. America owed its housing boom to China, because they want Americans to keep buying all that stuff they manufacture.

* Sometime in the next 10 years Brazil will probably pass the U.S. as the world's largest agricultural producer. Brazil is now the world's

largest exporter of chickens, orange juice, sugar, coffee, and tobacco. Last year, Brazil passed the U.S. as the world's largest beef producer. (Hear that cowboy?) As a result, while Americans bear record trade deficits, Brazil boasts a $30 billion trade surplus (NYT, Dec. 12, 2004).

* As of last June, the U.S. imported more food than it exported (NYT, Dec. 12, 2004).

* Bush: 62,027,582 votes. Kerry: 59,026,003 votes. Number of eligible voters who didn't show up: 79,279,000 (NYT, Dec. 26, 2004). That's more than a third. Way more. If more than a third of Iraqis didn't show for their election, no country in the world would think that election legitimate.

* One-third of all U.S. children are born out of wedlock. One-half of all U.S. children will live in a one-parent house (CNN, Dec. 10, 2004).

* "Americans are now spending more money on gambling than on movies, videos, DVDs, music, and books combined" (*The European Dream*, p.28).

* "Nearly one out of four Americans [believe] that using violence to get what they want is acceptable" (*The European Dream*, p.32).

* Forty-three percent of Americans think torture is sometimes justified, according to a PEW Poll (Associated Press, Aug. 19, 2004).

* "Nearly 900,000 children were abused or neglected in 2002, the last year for which such data are available" (USA Today, Dec. 21, 2004).

* "The International Association of Chiefs of Police said that cuts by the [Bush] administration in federal aid to local police agencies have left the nation more vulnerable than ever" (USA Today, Nov. 17, 2004).

* Defense spending has surged – up 60% from 2001 levels – and the official 2007 budget breakdown from the White House website confirmed the bulk of discretionary spending is headed for defense. The Pentagon is slated to get an 11% spending increase to $481 billion; $34 billion is allocated for Homeland Security; and an extra $245 billion for the Global War on Terror (if you include the supplemental requests for 2007).... three quarters of a *trillion* dollars, to flex muscle, dictate to the world and protect the American way?

America is No. 1? In most important categories, America is not even in the Top 10 anymore. Not even close.

My goal is not to denigrate America, but instead to wake up a few American souls to the propaganda and self-serving selling of America as the best and only way. Then, I believe, Americans might move to the next level of understanding and respect for other cultures and ways of life, instead of trying to beat the world into submission. If the American ideology is truly better than all else in the world, then the U.S. should be winning the hearts and minds of the world by ideas, and words and deeds, not by arms.

Would you like to live in a society of peace, prosperity and freedom? Would you like better opportunities for your children, like those you had growing up, to be free to do whatever you want so long as it doesn't harm others, and see the threats of violence and war largely disappear? Would you like to live in an age of artistic freedom and rapid scientific progress in which anything seems possible?

Such a world is not only possible - it is a part of your history. For nearly fifty years, between the end of the U.S. Civil War in 1865 and the beginning of World War I in 1914, the United States was the freest, most prosperous society on earth. Living standards rose nearly 5% every year. The average American's income was *six times* higher at the end of the period than at the beginning.

There was little restriction upon personal travel or economic and artistic freedom. There was no income tax, no military draft, little government regulation of business, and no prohibition of drugs.

Independent schools and private charities made education available for all, and helped those in need. In America, the nation enjoyed the longest period without foreign wars in its history except for the brief Spanish-American War. Nearly anything seemed possible. Illiterate immigrants who started with a pushcart became millionaires through hard work.

Today is different.

America and the world of the new millennium are far removed from the world of the past century, both in time and in spirit. Today's social landscape is one of deterioration, violence and mounting fear.

Take-home pay fell 17% between 1980 and 2007 when adjusting for inflation. High taxes and regulations are crippling America's economy. Few young adults can now afford to buy their own homes, save for their children's education, or build security for their retirement. And America is not alone as Australia, Great Britain and Europe follow closely behind in bureaucratic gobbledygook.

In America, violence has become epidemic. Murder is now the leading cause of death among young minority men. One in four college women report they were the victim of rape or attempted rape. And nearly 25% of all American families are now victimized by theft or vandalism every year.

Threats of weapons of mass destruction – chemical, biological and nuclear – continue to spread to the world's most repressive regimes, many of which have been historically supported by U.S. military and economic aid.

What has changed in America and the world, particularly during the last 50 years? Why has America changed from one of the most prosperous and progressive on earth to one of increasing deterioration and violence? America is declining because it has largely abandoned its *libertarian* heritage.

Thomas Jefferson, George Washington and America's other founders understood the values required for a free, peaceful and prosperous society: individual liberty, economic freedom, and limited government.

Liberty means the freedom to control your own life, to work and play as you choose, to keep what you earn, to practice the religion of your choice, to speak freely, and to associate voluntarily with others.

Liberty can flourish only in an environment of tolerance, voluntary association, and mutual respect for the lives and property of others. You can have liberty for yourself only if you grant it freely to everyone else.

The genius of America was that the government was created as a *protector* of your fundamental human rights. America's founders well understood that government's immense power can be used to destroy as well as to protect; that when government uses force against its own peaceful citizens, it becomes just another criminal gang. The Constitution and Bill of Rights was designed to protect Americans *from government.*

The libertarian ideal, that government exists to protect human rights, was never fully realized. American legislatures, police and military have frequently crossed the line from defenders of liberty to violators of it. But the previously slow erosion of human rights, your rights, has recently become a raging torrent, and the heritage of liberty is quickly being obliterated.

If you're typical, wherever you live, you now spend almost five months a year working to earn enough just to pay your taxes. And that's only the beginning. Added to that burden are the compliance costs for tax accountants, attorneys, tax software, etc.

When you add your income tax you pay directly in taxes, the amounts you pay indirectly in compliance costs, and the amounts you lose as a result of economic regulations, your *real* tax burden climbs to an enormous level that is now taken from you by the government.

In Los Angeles, it takes up to 70 licenses and permits to open a small business. In Washington, DC it costs $7,000 in fees to operate a push-cart. In New York City, a "medallion" to operate a taxicab costs over $150,000.

In Hawaii, a homeless man who tried to earn a little cash by taking pictures of tourists with his pet parrot, was arrested and his parrot confiscated because he didn't have a business license.

Over 50,000 pages of new regulations are now published in the Federal Register every year. That's in addition to *state* and *local* regulations.

Goods and services that could improve your life are being banned, confiscated, and regulated out of existence.

You no longer have a right to your own property. Over 200 federal and thousands of state civil asset forfeiture laws, authorize police to confiscate everything you own without trial or even without charging you with a crime.

Cars, homes, businesses, pocket cash, bank accounts, and pensions are now confiscated from thousands of *innocent* Americans every week. According to a Pittsburgh Press study, in 80% of the cases no one is ever charged with a crime.

Even if you are totally innocent of any crime, there is little chance you will ever get your confiscated property back. Under civil-forfeiture laws you are *presumed guilty,* and you must prove your innocence and pay staggering legal expenses out of your own pocket – *after* your home, bank accounts or business have been seized.

According to "60 Minutes," Oakland, California Housing Authority Police routinely rob public housing residents, plant drugs on them, beat them, and then arrest them. In Oakland, on an average night, 42 people are admitted to hospital emergency rooms after police beatings. But they're the lucky ones.

In California, "Multimillionaire rancher Donald Scott, 61, was shot to death when 26 DEA agents, LA County sheriff's deputies and National Park Service officers raided his 200-acre Malibu spread looking for marijuana they never found."

"Annie Rae Dixon, 84, bedridden with pneumonia in Tyler, Texas, [was] shot to death by police in a 2 a.m. raid. An officer said his pistol accidentally went off when he kicked down her bedroom door. No drugs were found." (Above quotes are from *USA Today*)

Now with the new war on terrorism, there are dozens of such deadly police "mistakes" every week. If an anonymous informant claims without proof that you have illegal drugs or firearms in your possession, that now gives police a virtual license to kill you and your family.

America must lead the way and return to the principles of tolerance and respect for the rights of others, at home and globally. Activities that are crimes for individuals – theft, assault, kidnapping, intimidation and murder – must be crimes for government agents and government representatives as well.

The crushing burden of confiscatory taxes and suffocating regulations must be lifted from the American economy and the rest of the global market place. Adding import duty taxes, more regulatory restrictions and protectionism measures is an immense step backwards.

As the revolutions that swept Eastern Europe and the Soviet Union demonstrated, even authoritarian governments require the consent of the governed. Sad to say, the same may be necessary in America if there is any hope of a better future.

America can again be the land of liberty and unlimited opportunity for the world to follow. This is what America once was and can be again. There is a movement afoot in America called Libertarians to restore America's liberties and freedom.... we can only hope it's not too little, too late.

Today, unfortunately, USA is "No. 1" in nothing but taxes, weaponry, consumer spending, debt, and delusion. Wake up, and rise above it, the world awaits you.

What luck for the rulers that men do not think.
Adolf Hitler

Epilogue

The world is filled with wonderful people, cultures, and new ways of doing things. Like Don Juan Ponce de Leon, maybe I too am looking for the fountain of youth so I can learn and live the many ways I could once only dream about. True, I have learned over the years that paradise is only found in one place, and that is in your mind. And as I am discovering, opening the mind, thinking, learning and living is as important as all else as you seek out your dreams in paradise.

I share with you the many legal and tax issues in this book not as obstacles standing in the way to a better life of living and investing offshore, but merely as "things" to plan around. Use the metaphor of walking through a tree lined forest on a sunny afternoon. If you close your eyes, you are certain to bump into plenty of trees, get bruised and probably end up getting lost. But if you open up your eyes and see the light through the trees, you can negotiate around the obstacles and hopefully avoid getting lost and experiencing the bruises along the way. And so to is moving and investing offshore.

Recently I addressed a group of 60 Americans at an International Living conference in New Zealand looking to live or invest, offshore. The age of the attendees varied between thirty and seventy, and their backgrounds represented an entire cross-spectrum of income levels, education and knowledge of what "offshore" means. What they all shared in common was a belief that they were not leaving America better for the next generation of children.... the American way had changed drastically over recent decades, and not necessarily for the better. The American dream was being sought after on foreign soils.

These forward thinking individuals at the Auckland conference were looking for choices that could make their lives better, and for some, better for their children. Their thirst for knowledge was evident as were the abundance of questions. I believe it is these pioneering spirits that will have an upper hand for a more promising, fulfilling future.

I hope that this book allows you to see a little better through the maze of trees in the forest. My goal in sharing the thoughts on these pages, and in *"How to Legally Protect Your Assets"*, has been to provide a road map to personal and financial independence to live a sovereign life. If I have shed some light – and your knowledge and understanding of the world is more transparent – then we have both succeeded in our missions.

I still provide a limited amount of private consulting on the legal topics covered in these two books, but refer tax issues to those better equipped than I on the topic. If your intentions are honorable, and if you are considering *"offshore"*, I would enjoy hearing about your plans and exploring if I can assist in your endeavors with pre-migration planning, wealth preservation or asset protection planning. A team approach is a good approach......... and perhaps together we can find the pieces that fit.

"The superior man, when resting in safety,
does not forget that danger may come."
Confucius

ABOUT THE AUTHOR

Following over thirty years in law and business, David Tanzer now concentrates in International Consulting for clients located around the world. David provides guidance to individuals and businesses, assisting them in mitigating personal and business risks, migrating "offshore", allowing for opportunities for wealth preservation, asset protection, and growth.

As a past Adjunct Professor of Law, former Judge, and retired commercial litigation attorney, David has seen wealth exchange hands quickly for litigants who have failed to take proper planning steps. *"Too often,"* says Tanzer, *"a client will seek strategies to reduce losses only after they are already confronted with a problem. Then, it may be too late and damage control is about all that is left."* Tanzer places emphasis on advance planning steps before a problem materializes.

"A key part of successful planning is to take necessary steps today, before a problem arises." Bringing together international contacts in the disciplines of law, tax and business is an integral part of the planning process.

David Tanzer is a member of the Offshore Institute, a multidisciplinary international professional organization of individuals engaged in offshore and international planning. David is on the Wealth Advisory Panel of the Oxford Club, a private, international organization of investors and entrepreneurs.

As a litigation attorney, David won a number of large civil lawsuits and is a member in a national trial lawyers group set up to recognize such milestone financial awards – the Million Dollar Advocates Forum.

Started in 1993, the forum honors trial lawyers *"whose skill, experience and excellence in Advocacy"* have won them verdicts or settlements of $1 million or more. The forum has about 300 members, from more than 800,000 attorneys in the United States. David Tanzer is proud to be one of the very few attorneys who are qualified members of the Million Dollar Advocates Forum.

David Tanzer earned his Bachelor of Science at De Paul University graduating with High Honors in Finance at Chicago, Illinois. By invitation, he was installed as a member of Delta Mu Delta, a national honorary society in business administration. He then went on to study law, receiving his Juris Doctorate at IIT-Kent School of Law.

Thereafter, David returned to DePaul as an Adjunct Professor of Law teaching law and finance. He also served by appointment on the bench in the Circuit Court of Cook County, Illinois as Chairman of Judicial Arbitration Panel for five years, one of the world's largest trial dockets. He also holds an Honorary Doctorate of Philosophy in Religions of the World.

David has tried complex civil cases, developing special expertise in business and transactional law, commercial litigation, asset protection and wealth preservation. After entering private law practice he became a named partner in the law firm of Bjork, Tanzer & Associates, Ltd. in Chicago, Illinois, and then later on relocated his practice to Vail, Colorado, establishing the law firm David A. Tanzer & Associates, PC.

Tanzer is also a present or former member of the Colorado Bar Association Judiciary Executive Counsel, the American Bar Association, Chicago Bar Association, Northwest Bar Association, Association of Trial Lawyers of America, and the Continental Divide Bar Association. He is also an Associate Member of the Auckland District Law Society, New Zealand and an Associate Member of the Queensland Law Society, Australia.

The author of the book *"How to Legally Protect Your Assets"*, and numerous articles on international business and asset protection planning, David Tanzer is a sought after speaker on topics of international asset protection planning and wealth preservation.

David now specializes in helping people like you to learn the many techniques of how to protect and preserve assets. For more information visit **www.DavidTanzer.com**.

David Tanzer is licensed to Practice Law in U.S. States & Federal Courts;
Assoc. Member Auckland, N.Z. District Law Society - Foreign Lawyer;
& Assoc. Member Queensland Law Society, AU - Foreign Lawyer.

Datlegal@aol.com

OUR DISCLAIMERS

Every individual situation has different circumstances and will lead to different outcomes on which specific legal, taxation, accounting and other relevant advice must be taken. No reliance should be made on any part of the contents nor is any responsibility accepted by the author, the publisher or anyone else associated with the book, nor can proceedings be brought in any jurisdiction or under any law, of that jurisdiction or otherwise.

To the contrary, this publication is intended to provide or to include a non-technical explanation of certain legal, tax and compliance concepts for general informational purposes only. It is sold with the understanding that neither the authors nor the publisher are engaged in rendering any legal, tax, accounting, investment or other professional services to or for the reader. If legal, tax, accounting investment or other professional advice is required, the services of a qualified professional person should be sought.

The information herein does not constitute authoritative support for any tax matter discussed herein. The only sources of authoritative support for tax matters are pertinent sections of the U.S. Tax Code, the Internal Revenue Code, IRS Regulations, rulings or technical advice memoranda and any court cases that bear on the subject matter.

Further, this report is not a reliance opinion or a marketed opinion. This report and its contents were not intended or written by the author to be used, and cannot be used, by anyone for the purpose of (i) avoiding U.S. tax penalties, or (ii) promoting, marketing or recommending to another party any transaction or mailer addressed or stated herein. This book and its contents are not treated as a marketed opinion because (a) the advice was not intended or written to be used, and it cannot be used by any taxpayer, for the purpose of avoiding penalties that may be imposed on the taxpayer; (b) the advice was not written to support the promotion or marketing of the transaction(s) or matter(s) addressed herein; and (c) the taxpayer should seek advice based on the taxpayer's particular circumstances from an independent tax advisor. [31 C.F.R. sections 1O.35(b)(4)(ii); 1O.35(b)(5)(i); and (b)(5)(ii)(a), (b) and (c).]

The comments in this book are not intended to constitute an opinion regarding any specific legal or tax issues because additional facts and issues may exist that could affect the legal or tax treatment of the issues addressed in this book. This book does not consider or reach conclusion with respect to those additional issues and was not written and cannot be used for the purpose of avoiding penalties under code section 6662(d).

A special thank you to Vern Jacobs and Offshore Press for information found in segments of this book regarding tax issues. For more information on the U.S. tax treatment of U.S. investors see www.offshorepress.com

Index

NOTES

NOTES

NOTES